Caught in the Crossfire

Georgia L. Barnes-Payne

Payne Prairie

Publications

Payne Prairie

Publications

Caught in the Crossfire

For information address: Payne Prairie Publications

215 N McColm, Bolivar, MO 65613

PRINTING HISTORY

First Printing 1997
Second Printing 2019

PPP books are published by Payne Prairie Publications

215 N McColm, Bolivar, MO 65613

The name "PPP" and the "PPP" logo are trademarks belonging to Payne Prairie Publications

ISBN: 978-0761000655

PRINTED IN THE UNITED STATES OF AMERICA

This book is dedicated posthumously to my parents,
Dorothy L. and G. Sheldon Barnes,
whose courage and unerring instinctive actions brought their family through a
very dangerous situation. I owe them my life.

Acknowledgments

I wish to thank my husband, Gervais, without whose support this book would not be. My two sons, Lendon and David, and their wives, Marja-Liisa and Ann, respectively, have given unfailing editorial assistance and headed up a cheering section on which I could rely. My sister-in-law, Bobbie Barnes, has spent countless hours at my elbow with patient encouragement as well as at the word processor. Many friends, relatives, and neighbors have urged perseverance whenever hope failed me. Thanks to all.

Prologue

Wiping the chocolate frosting off my knuckles, I took one last swipe over the top of the cake with a spatula and stood back for a look. The cake was slightly lopsided, but there wasn't time to make another one. It would have to do for our little family get-together. My brother, Pete, turned twenty earlier in the week, and the next day my parents marked another milestone in their marriage. Today the whole family was gathering at the folks' house to celebrate with a cookout. Little did I know that we would be celebrating still another happy occasion.

I peeked over the newspaper at my husband. "It's time to get the car out. And see if the boys are ready. If we don't hurry, we'll be the last ones there."

With our two sons in the back seat and the cake held carefully on my lap, we started across town. My folks lived in Independence, Missouri, about a twenty-minute ride away. It was a beautiful fall day, quite cool in the shade but warm in the sun. The sky was a deep sparkling blue, the kind we see in Kansas City only when the humidity is low. A kaleidoscope of bright oranges, reds, and yellows glittered from the wooded bluff above the Missouri River.

When we arrived, Mom was in the kitchen as usual. I gave her a big hug. "Some of your special potato salad?"

"You keep telling me we can't have a cookout without it." She smiled. "How are you, hon?"

"Just fine. Dad on the deck?" I asked, moving in that direction. "Yes, and everyone else except Pete," she called. Just as I thought, Dad was already starting a bed of charcoal for the hamburgers. There was nothing either one of the folks enjoyed more than having their family come to visit. Cooking for all of us now seemed to give them special pleasure since there was no limit on what or how much they could fix; a marked difference from our years in prison camp.

"You must be a friend of the weatherman, Dad," I said, patting him on the shoulder. "It couldn't be more lovely."

Dad grinned. "I pulled a few strings." He could be a pixie sometimes, with a wry sense of humor.

My sister, Carole, and I hugged each other, and then she pushed me away and said, "Let me look at my big sister." The oldest of four, albeit the smallest, I took a lot of ribbing about my size.

"Should I look different today?" I asked, puzzled.

"Well, I thought someone so close to her thirty-third birthday would just naturally look older than she did this summer," Carole teased.

Mother came out of the house just then and clapped her hands. "Attention, everybody. Pete's here now. Dad and I already know about the surprise he has for the rest of you."

Pete stepped onto the porch, followed closely by a blond girl gripping his hand tightly. Always reticent, like Dad, Pete looked, more than usual, at a loss for words. The girl seemed dismayed by the sight of so many strangers.

"This is Bobbie," Pete finally managed to say, pulling her closer. "Bobbie and I were married on my birthday."

The surprise struck us all mute momentarily, but finally Carole said, "Welcome to the family, Bobbie." Then everyone crowded around the newlyweds, each with their own greeting. Pete took the requisite teasing good-naturedly. The warmth of our welcome slowly eased the uncertainty from Bobbie's face to be replaced by the pleasant smile we have since come to know reflects her true nature.

Our family gathering, like so many others before it, progressed from teasing and laughing to playing games with the children and quiet one-on-one conversations. As always, Dad and Mom, Carole, and I would make a few comments about camp. When we did, the others would fall silent and listen intently to the snippets of information that crept out. Over the years my husband had found it necessary to piece together the story of my years in camp from such casual bits. For me, talking about the whole experience from start to finish was still too difficult; I'd break out in a sweat, my hands would shake, and my voice took on a noticeable quaver.

Still, when the four of us were together, it seemed we could not leave the topic alone. Perhaps it made life in the present a little sweeter by reviewing, however briefly, those dangerous and trying times twenty years earlier.

Carole and her family left by midafternoon. They needed to be home, some fifty miles away, in time to do their farm chores before dark. It was almost time for us to go as well. The boys wanted to be home in time to watch their favorite Sunday-night television shows.

While I was getting our jackets out of the closet, Bobbie came over to me.

"Georgia, I'd sure like to know more about the camp you and your folks talk about. Pete has mentioned it a few times, but I know I don't have the full story."

"Well, he was too small to remember anything about camp," I answered quickly.

"I know it was a Japanese prisoner-of-war camp and it was called Santo Tomas, but that's about all I know. Please tell me about it," she urged.

"Maybe we can get together sometime for a chat, just you and I." I felt myself relenting. "It bothers me so much to talk to large groups of people that I just don't do it anymore. But if . . ." I paused.

"Wednesday is my usual day off," Bobbie volunteered.

She was obviously not to be denied. Any further sidestepping would have seemed unfriendly, and that wasn't the way I wanted our new sisterly relationship to begin. I liked her already. "Well then," I agreed hesitantly, "come Wednesday morning about nine and I'll fill you in on some of our family history."

Wednesday rolled around, bringing with it dark and chilly weather; a good morning to stay in and sip hot tea with my new sister-in-law. The teakettle was singing on the stove, and the sugar bowl and creamer were filled. But before I could fix a plate of cookies, the doorbell rang. Bobbie was early and apparently eager for a more thorough introduction to her new family.

Settled on the sofa with our mugs of steaming brew, I hardly had a moment to catch my breath before the questions started coming.

"What kind of a camp were you in?" Bobbie began.

"It was a civilian concentration camp in World War II," I answered slowly, not knowing at first if she would be interested in much detail.

"Where were you, for heaven's sake?" she wondered aloud.

"In the Philippine Islands."

I found our world atlas and turned to the western Pacific to show her where it was. On such a vast ocean, the Philippines seemed small and insignificant. I had to marvel, just for a moment myself, at the chain of events which led to our being caught in the middle of a world war in such a remote spot.

"You mean you were actually prisoners during the war?" Bobbie's face was changing. The pleasant smile was slipping away. In its place was a growing look of incredulity.

"Yes." That old, familiar shaky feeling was creeping over me. My hand trembled so that I had to set my tea down. My heart felt like it was beating in the hollow at the base of my throat. Why, after some twenty intervening years, was this still happening to me? Would I ever be able to talk dispassionately about that period in my life? I knew that many people, once they learned about my experiences, were genuinely interested in hearing as many details as I would give them. A few people, not wanting to pry or rake open old wounds I'm sure, would show no outward interest at all. Paradoxically, this, too, was hard for me to cope with—as if that period behind walls were no more significant than a day at the beach. While I sat struggling to regain some measure of inner calm, I could see Bobbie might be a little confused about that place and time in history. After all, she was fifteen years my junior and not even alive at the time I was talking about.

Finally, she exploded with a torrent of questions.

"Prisoners for how long? What was it like? Why in the world were you there in the first place?"

"Hold on," I laughed, feeling myself relax a bit. "How about if I start at the beginning and we take this in easy stages? We could even do this several Wednesdays."

"That's fine with me," Bobbie readily agreed. "This is beginning to sound like a horror story, and yet I'm fascinated. Whenever you're ready," she prompted me.

Staring into my teacup, I took my time sorting through all the thoughts, recollections, and wisps of memory that I could call upon to relate a historically accurate and chronologically coherent story. This recounting of our family history was taking place in the fall of 1961. For Bobbie's sake, I needed to make sense of a story that started not only before she was born, but even before I was born. After a few moments, I decided to begin my tale at the opening of the twentieth century.

Chapter 1

The United States fought and won a war against Spain in 1898. As a result of that war, Spain lost the island of Cuba in the Caribbean Sea and the Philippine Islands in the western Pacific Ocean. Within a year or two following that victory, the American government advertised for American citizens interested in living and working in the newly won territory. My dad's parents, being young and adventurous, answered the call. The newlyweds accepted jobs as civil-service teachers in Manila, the capital city of the Philippines. My grandparents boarded ship in California and sailed across the vast Pacific, arriving in Manila sometime after the middle of 1905. Dad's older brother, my Uncle Dick, was born on that voyage. Dad was born in Manila in late 1906.

The family adjusted to the local lifestyle and lived there comfortably for many years. When Dad was about fourteen years old, his parents decided that he and his brother should return to the States in order to complete their education. It was to Lawrence, Kansas, that the boys were taken to study in an Indian boarding school, where their mother had been a student and their grandmother a teacher. Dad and his brother spent occasional weekends and holidays visiting relatives in the Kansas City area.

Uncle Dick, of course, finished his high school work first and left to pursue higher education elsewhere. Dad, without his brother there, became dissatisfied and lonely. Taking responsibility for his own actions, Dad left school and went to live with a favorite uncle in Independence, Missouri. There he worked for several years at various jobs, not really making a mark for himself, but keeping body and soul together in the roaring twenties.

About 1926 or 1927 Dad met my mother at a church social. They were married in October, 1928. At first they were able to have an apartment of their own as both of them had jobs. Dad was a swimming instructor at the Kansas City YMCA and Mother was an illustrator for Hallmark Cards. Exactly one year later, the worst economic depression this country had ever known began with the stock market crash on Wall Street. I was born one month later, in November, 1929. I don't know how long Dad was able to keep working, but Mother had not worked for a while before I was born.

The first casualty of the depression for the young family was the loss of their apartment; they moved in with Mother's folks. When Dad lost his job, the only person employed in the household was Mother's father, my grandad Haley. Fortunately, his job was secure. It was a sign of those difficult times, that a man nearing retirement age would be the sole support for a family of five. By early 1931, the household grew to six when my sister, Carole, was born. Dad searched endlessly, but fruitlessly, for work.

In 1934 a letter arrived from Dad's mother in Manila promising him a job there. His parents had divorced many years earlier. His mother was remarried to a wealthy businessman who was influential in securing jobs in the Philippines for both of her sons. Dad jumped at the chance; anything at all would be better than to continue living on the largesse of his in-laws. Money to pay our passage was wired from Manila.

So the Barnes family set sail for Manila. Carole was three years old then, and I was four and a half. I don't remember much about the voyage except that I was frequently tied into a large chair and given my "knitting" to do while the folks kept track of Carole.

On arrival, we soon settled into our new life. Living in the tropics required becoming accustomed to typhoons, monsoons, sweltering summers, earthquakes, and a whole new array of bodily ailments. Nevertheless, Manila, in a short while, supplanted Kansas City in my heart and mind as home. Dad, as promised, was hired as an insurance adjuster.

Uncle Dick was already working as a mining engineer at a gold mine on one of the remote southern islands. In 1937, he married Evelyn Crew and was transferred to another mine north of Manila, where she accompanied him. We seldom saw them, because they came to Manila only rarely for shopping trips or brief vacations. It was much too arduous a trip for a family with small children to visit them at the mine.

In 1939, after being in the Philippines for five years, we were sent home to Kansas City for a long visit. At that time the United States government required all of its citizens to abide in the country for at least six months after every five years in a foreign land. Kansas City's winter was a shock to all of us after so many years in the tropics. The lengthy, rewarding visit with loved ones notwithstanding, we were ready to go back to Manila when the vacation was over in the spring of 1940.

As early as 1935 the rattle of sabers could be heard in the Far East when Japan invaded China. Then in 1939 Hitler's Germany invaded Poland. As we prepared to leave the States again some voices were being raised concerning the possibility of the war in Europe spreading to join the conflict in the Far East, thus becoming a world war. There did not appear to us to be any urgent reason to heed those voices; we were average American citizens not privy to the worrisome information beginning to pile up on desks at the State Department.

We sailed west from California free of cares.

In April 1940, halfway across the Pacific, our ship's captain received a news cable that gave everyone on board some cause for worry. Hitler had invaded Norway. Our captain quickly ordered his crew to paint over all the ship's flags and insignia. We were sailing on a Norwegian ship! The voyage, however, proved to be uneventful, and we arrived safely in Manila.

For the next eighteen months there were a number of local and world events that should have caused us to pause and take stock of our situation. British refugees from China began to arrive in Manila. Dutch nationals were fleeing the Japanese invasion of the East Indies. The Unites States Army and Navy were sending home many of the military wives and children from bases around the Far East.

For some reason, American civilians in the Philippines were neither ordered to leave nor warned of impending peril. The general population of the Philippines, Hawaii, and the United States had no idea that war was imminent. Certainly the Barnes family, domiciled in Manila, did not guess. Perhaps a few officials in the inner sanctums of Washington, D.C. could have predicted, if pressed, that our nation was already headed for a collision with war on a worldwide scale. The inevitable impact would occur on a peaceful Sunday morning, December 7, 1941, in Hawaii.

Because the International Dateline runs north and south between Hawaii and the Philippines, our family in Manila heard news of the bombing of Pearl Harbor only a few hours after it occurred, but the day was Monday, December 8, not Sunday the 7th.

That fateful day started no differently than hundreds of other days spent at Bordner School. Mrs. Sylvester's voice was making me sleepy in the stifling classroom. Across the aisle. Julio was already nodding. Even the flies buzzing around the ceiling fan were moving as if through thick honey in the muggy air. Sweat beaded on my forehead and pasted tendrils of hair to my neck as I sat doodling drowsily on my chalkboard. My thoughts, diverted from schoolwork, wandered out the large open window.

Four lanes of traffic on Taft Avenue rumbled past the school. Dust and noise wafted through the window on the faintest of breezes as Filipino drivers yelled insults at each other in their native language. Mother would have been horrified to know I could understand some of them! Too often the crack of a whip could be heard above the general din, and then I knew the little horses pulling carriages were being harshly treated. Their drivers were wont to overload the carts and then whip the luckless beasts to go faster.

The week promised to be another long one, and even after that, it would be two more weeks before the Christmas vacation. At the age of twelve, I wished devoutly for that time to pass quickly. Thus dreamily occupied, it may have been several minutes before I realized the teacher was no longer talking. When I looked around to see why, I saw Dad standing in the doorway.

He looked so nice in the white linen business suit customarily worn in the tropics. Dad was a handsome man with finely cut features, blond hair, and greenish-gray eyes.

A slender build and healthy tan gave testimony to his love of swimming and sailing.

After speaking to the teacher for a moment longer, Dad looked toward me and beckoned. Mrs. Sylvester excused me from class for the rest of the day.

"Why, Dad?" I asked, catching hold of his hand as he turned to leave. "Is Mother all right?" I was naturally happy to be leaving class, but Dad looked so worried it bothered me.

"Yes, she's fine," he answered, walking quickly down the hall. "Let's go get Sis."

As we strode to Mrs. Baker's fourth-grade room, I began to notice other parents in the hall. All of them certainly seemed in a hurry. Why, there went Carole's friend Rosemary with her mother toward the front door.

Carole was standing by her seat, reciting to the class. When she saw Dad and me, my sister's eyebrows went straight up in surprise, and a little worry frown crinkled the space between. Dad stepped into the room and said something to the teacher, while I motioned for Carole to put away her books. She, too, was excused from class.

Back down the hall, Dad set a quick pace. "Let's go home now," he said. "Mother is waiting for us."

When Dad used that tone of voice, it was best not to risk a sharp look by asking questions. So Carole and I rode home quietly in the backseat of the company car, but we whispered back and forth to each other.

"What could be so important as to bring Dad, himself, to fetch us?"

"Why couldn't he have sent one of the servants?"

"Wonder why he isn't at work today."

"So many other kids were leaving school too!"

"Something very unusual is going on."

In this way we spent the time on the short ride home. Our home in Manila was a spacious apartment that took up half of the second floor of a three-story building. The address, 1034 Indiana Street, was in the district of Malate. It was an old, lovely part of town where such buildings as ours were sparsely scattered among stately homes that dated from Spanish colonial days. Most of those estates were surrounded by carefully kept formal gardens and enclosed by stone or wrought-iron fences. The owners usually kept large, ferocious dogs to deter sneak thieves.

As Dad pulled up and parked in front of our building, the Doberman next door came rushing up to the fence, barking and growling in a terrible show of might. But when we climbed out of the car he began wagging his tail.

"Oh, Bosco," Carole scolded, "you should know this car by now. You wouldn't bite us, would you?" Reaching through the fence, she patted him on the head.

"Sheldon," Mother called down from our veranda, "there's a special newscast from San Francisco on the radio right now, but I can't get it to come through clearly."

"I'll be right up, Dorothy," Dad replied. "Come on, girls. Hurry! Let's catch that news."

We all gathered around the shortwave radio while Dad tried to tune out the static. Several minutes passed and then he said, "Guess we'll have to give up on San Francisco for right now and try a local station."

". . . interrupt this regularly scheduled program to summarize the news for those of you who have just tuned in. A Japanese naval task force in an early-morning attack today struck at the United States' military installations in Hawaii. Reports are still sketchy, but it appears as if many of the American ships at anchor in Pearl Harbor were sunk or severely damaged. No accurate count of the casualties can be made at this point, but it is estimated that hundreds, if not thousands, have been killed or wounded.

"Simultaneously, the Japanese launched similar raids on Hickam Air Force Base and Schofield Army Barracks, both in the area near Pearl Harbor. So little warning did the Americans have that nearly all of the planes at Hickam were caught on the ground and destroyed. Many of the men at Hickam and Schofield were wounded or killed in a valiant attempt to defend their bases against overwhelming odds."

Carole and I instinctively moved closer to Dad and Mother. "Hawaii isn't very far away, is it?" I asked.

"Shhh," Dad motioned with a finger on his lips.

While the folks stared numbly at the radio, the announcer continued. ". . . evil deed was carried out at the same time Japanese envoys were negotiating with United States officials in Washington, D.C. The Japanese government has, for some time, tried to convince Western Pacific interests that it did not pose a threat in this part of the world. But now the evil intentions of Prime Minister Tojo and his cabinet can be seen in their true light.

"Please stay tuned. We will break in with further developments as they become available. Later today we hope to have a statement from the High Commissioner's office as to how these events may affect us here in Manila. It is safe to say now, though, that the United States will most certainly declare war on Japan, in which event we here in the Philippine Islands will be drawn into the conflict."

"What does it all mean, Dad?" I asked.

Before speaking he cleared his throat several times; it was a nervous habit of Dad's when he was carefully choosing just the right words. "Let's not worry about it until after lunch," he finally said, looking to Mother for confirmation.

Carole and I turned to Mother now. It would be she who would let us know, by voice and action, just how serious the situation really was. Dad was always so quietly reserved that it was sometimes difficult to judge an event by his reaction to it. Mother, on the other hand, was a lighthearted and outgoing woman. Her dark, curly hair framed a pretty face with deep brown eyes and a generous mouth that smiled easily. Her usual sprightly cheerfulness, however, was nowhere in evidence today.

"That's a good idea," she agreed soberly. "Why don't you girls go see if Pascencia is ready to serve? It is well past lunchtime now."

All afternoon Mother and Dad stayed close to the radio. They didn't even take their usual siesta, though Carole and I had to. Afterward, when we asked if we could go over to visit with Rosemary, we were told we must stay close to home. So we went out back to the servants' quarters. It was one of our favorite places to while away an hour or so. Behind our apartment house was a courtyard with a row of garages on the far side—one for each of the six apartments in our building. Above the garages was a row of rooms. Each apartment-dweller could have one of these rooms for his servants. All the rooms were connected by a common walkway across the front, with a single set of stairs at one end. Under the stairs was the laundry shed, which consisted of a concrete slab and a cold-water spigot.

It was there we went, and we were in luck. Aurora, our laundress, was doing the family wash. She was squatting on her haunches as usual and beating the wet clothes briskly with a wooden paddle. Deftly turning and folding the clothes, she beat them in a steady rhythm. Each blow sent a cooling spray of water our way that felt good on a warm day. But that was only one reason why we liked to watch her. Another was because Aurora was so much fun. She was an old woman who spoke hardly any English, but she enjoyed teasing us by an ingenuous use of gestures. She would compliment me on a new dress, for instance, by preening and bowing in an elaborate way and then smile toothlessly as she felt the material.

Aurora especially liked to horrify us by turning her indispensable brown cigarette around so that the burning end was inside her mouth. This would cause smoke to issue forth from her nostrils, and with wisps of gray hair streaming about as she worked, it was not hard for me to imagine her a witch pounding roots for a poisonous brew. And then she would wink and cackle wildly with amusement.

By the end of the day some sense of normalcy returned to our lives. We had dinner as usual. Afterward Dad treated us to a very special evening by reading aloud from a book of poetry. By bedtime I had all but forgotten the distressing newscasts of the day.

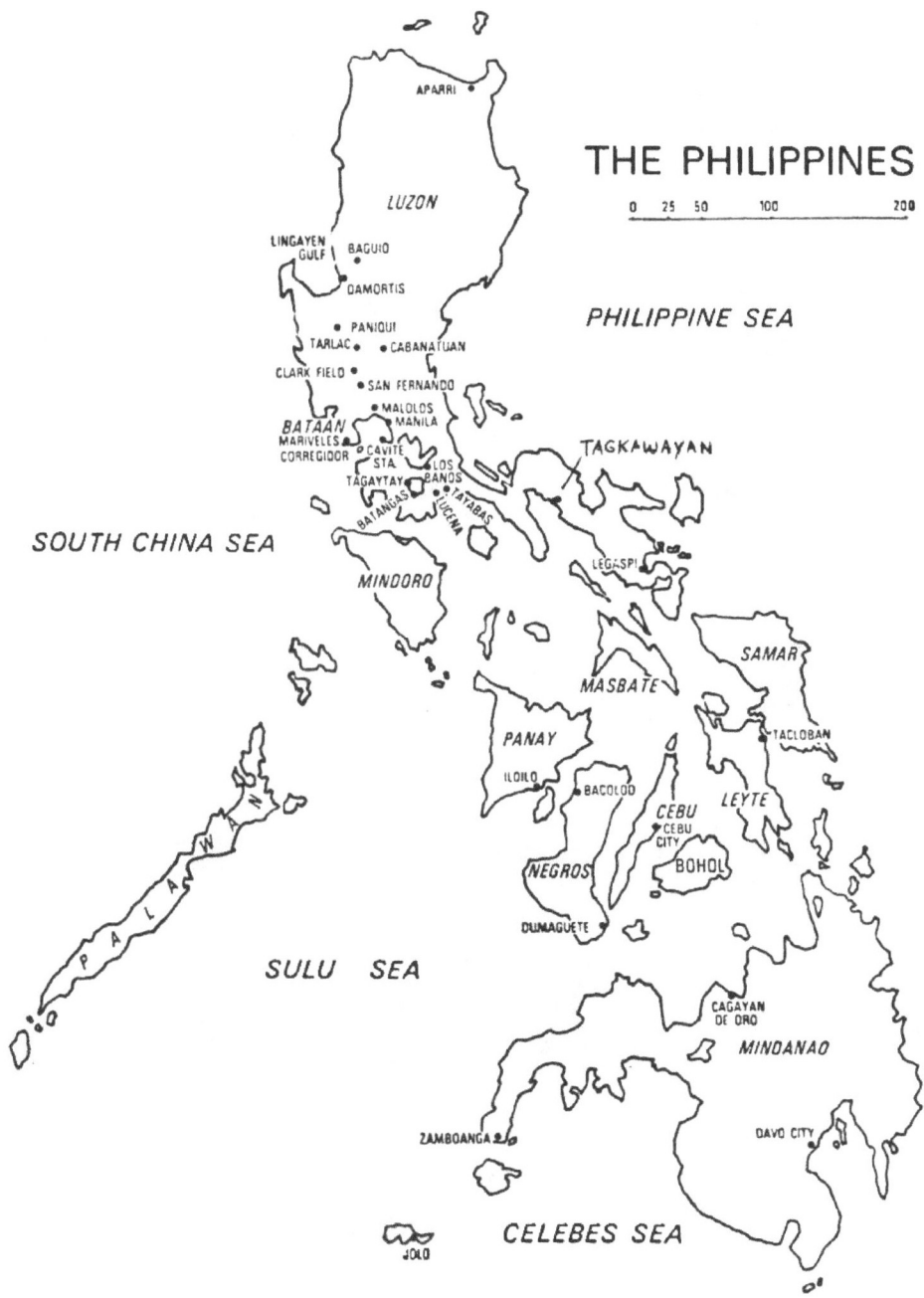

THE PHILIPPINES

0 25 50   100   200

APARRI

LUZON

PHILIPPINE SEA

LINGAYEN
GULF   BAGUIO

DAMORTIS

PANIQUI
TARLAC   • CABANATUAN
CLARK FIELD •
• SAN FERNANDO

MALOLOS
MANILA
BATAAN
MARIVELES
CORREGIDOR CAVITE
STA.
LOS
TAGAYTAY BANOS
BATANGAS LUCENA
TAYABAS

TAGKAWAYAN

SOUTH CHINA SEA

LEGASPI

MINDORO

SAMAR

MASBATE

PANAY

TACLOBAN

ILOILO
BACOLOD   LEYTE

CEBU
CEBU
CITY

NEGROS   BOHOL

DUMAGUETE

SULU   SEA

CAGAYAN
DE ORO

MINDANAO

ZAMBOANGA

DAVO CITY

CELEBES SEA

JOLO

*A.V.H. Hartendorp, *The Santo Tomas Story* (McGraw-Hill, 1964)

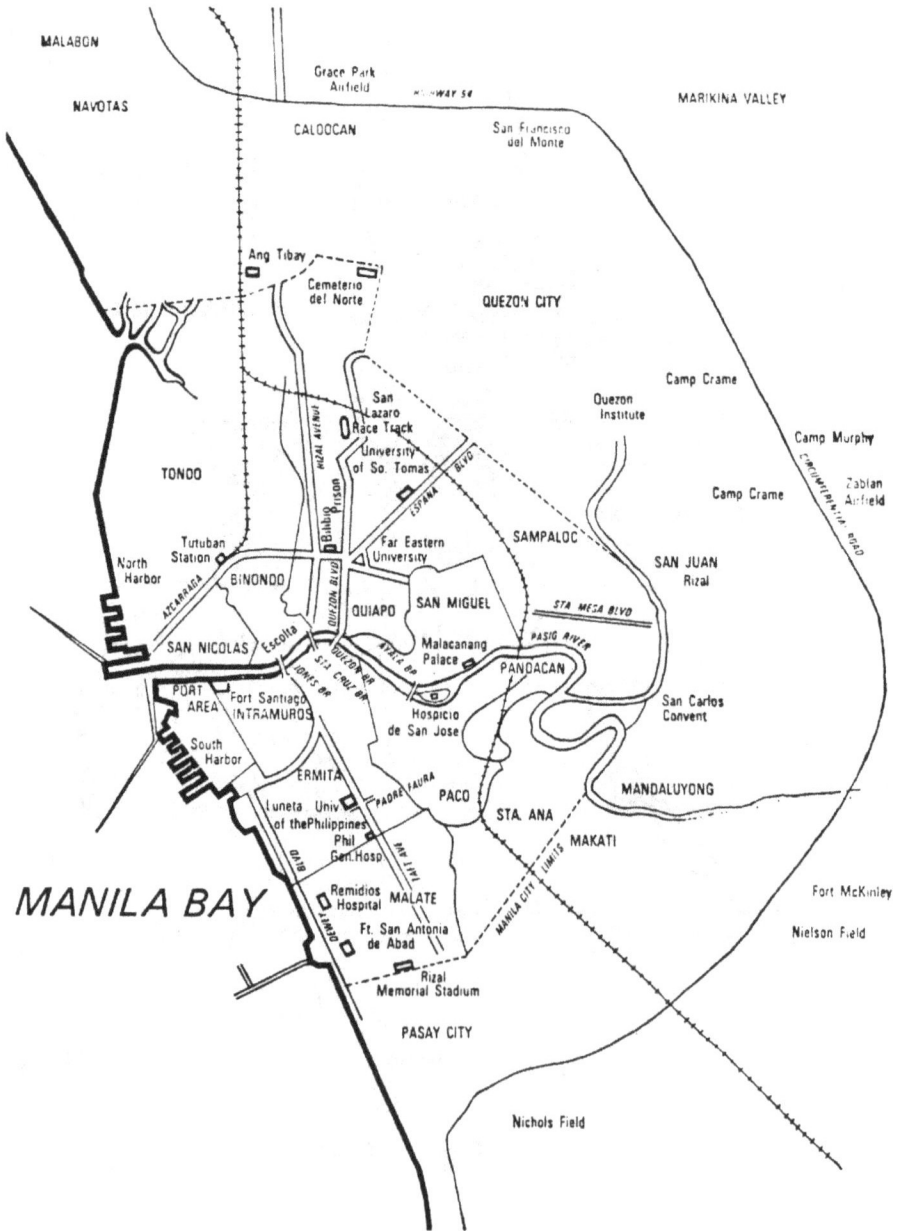

MANILA BAY

*A.V.H. Hartendorp, *The Santo Tomas Story* (McGraw-Hill, 1964)

Chapter 2

"Georgia, wake up!" Mother said, shaking my shoulder.

"Huh?" I mumbled, opening my eyes. It was pitch dark.

"Come with me, hon," she urged, taking me by the arm.

"Where are we going?" I whispered. "I can't see."

Just then a flashlight lit the space between my bed and Carole's. "Georgia, you go with Mother," Dad told me. "I'll bring Sis."

"What was that?" I almost yelled as a distant boom rattled the windows.

"Hurry," Dad said as we scurried down the hall and into the bathroom. He led Carole over against the far wall and motioned us both to sit down there. The folks sat as close on either side as they could, scrunching us all together. Several booms, this time much closer, rattled the bottles in the medicine cabinet. "I'm scared," Carole breathed, echoing my own feelings.

Almost certain of the answer I would get, I still had to ask: "What are those heavy sounds that rattle everything, Dad?"

"They're probably a mix of bombs and explosions of gasoline and oil tanks." Dad was trying so hard not to frighten us that he almost made being bombed sound like an ordinary occurrence.

"It's the Japanese, isn't it?" I asked, my voice rising a bit in spite of myself. "And they're doing to us just what they did to the Americans in Pearl Harbor, aren't they?"

"It sure sounds like it," Mother answered grimly.

Now the explosions were coming constantly. Some were near enough to keep things in the house rattling all the time. When there was a lull nearby we could hear the dull thud of bombs exploding in the distance.

"Why are we sitting here in the bathroom?" Carole's voice was all atremble. "Because there is only a small window in here," Dad answered matter-of-factly. "We don't want to be where there is a lot of flying glass."

Mother said, "Here, Georgia, why don't you put your head on my lap. Carole can put her head on Dad's, and maybe you girls can go back to sleep while we wait this out."

The tile floor didn't seem so hard with my head cradled this way. Sounds of the bombing drifted away as Dad and Mother started to softly sing some of the popular songs from their childhood and growing-up years. Their voices blended together so beautifully that I thought it the loveliest music in the world. I tried to stay awake just so I wouldn't miss any, but the singing worked its intended magic and I dozed.

Sometime during that long night, a bomb landed so close that Mother jumped. It jarred me into a semiwakeful state where I was not so much aware of the continuing bombing as I was of my folks no longer singing. They were talking earnestly in low tones.

The words *war* and *enemy* and *invasion* whirled around in my half dream and might have frightened me but for the gentle hand resting on my head.

I don't know how long the enemy planes wreaked their havoc on Manila, but by first light they were gone and we were packing suitcases. Dad had decided that Manila was not a safe place for Mother, Carole, and me. He felt the wisest thing for us to do would be to go visit his brother and sister-in-law at their home in the province of Camarines Norte, south of Manila. The three of us would go by ourselves because Dad still had his job at the insurance company to think of. A quick breakfast after the packing was finished and we were ready.

As we drove north across town toward Tutuban Railroad Station, we could see the smoke of fires in the Cavite Naval Station area. To the east, columns of black smoke billowed up from the Pandacan oil refinery. When we crossed the Pasig River we could see downstream to the port area; it looked as if every ship moored in Manila Bay was afire. The acrid smell of smoke grew stronger the farther we drove. In fact, the whole city reminded me of newsreels of the war in Europe, which we had seen at the movie theater.

Nearing the train station, we realized we weren't the only ones in Manila planning to flee the city. The plaza in front of the depot was crowded with vehicles of all sorts and hundreds of people shoving and pushing their way toward the entrance. Everyone was yelling or talking in a highly agitated way. It was a dangerous crowd with but one thought: to leave the terror of bombing behind them.

Using a mixture of Spanish, English, and the native dialect, Dad was able to get us inside the station. The crush became almost unbearable. Carole and I were wedged in so tightly, between Dad in front with the bags and Mother behind us, that we could hardly breathe! Faces of wild alarm and the frenzied babble of voices made me wish fervently that we had not left the tranquility of home. Our progress toward the ticket counter was agonizingly slow. That we moved at all was probably due, in part, to the way Dad was swinging those bags.

Finally, with tickets in hand, we passed through the gate into the train yard. Dodging this way and that, we picked our way through the hurrying throng and came at last to our railroad car. Dad stowed our bags on the wooden rack above our seats.

Other people clambered on board, filling all the remaining seats and then jamming the aisle. The train lurched, then began to move slowly.

Dad hugged us quickly as he said, "Girls, I want you to mind your mother in everything she says." Looking at first one of us and then the other, he asked, "Do I have your promises?"

"Yes, Dad," we said solemnly with one voice.

Turning to Mother, Dad said with perfect confidence, "If this train can get out of the city before another air raid starts, I'm sure the rest of the trip will be all right." He kissed her and then added, "I'll wire Porter that you're coming." Porter was the name everyone in the family, except Carole and I, called Uncle Dick.

By now the train was moving a little faster, so Dad pushed his way through to the door and jumped nimbly down onto the platform. As we waved to him, I thought he looked somewhat relieved; he had, after all, done what he thought was best for us. I wondered how soon all the scary war business would be over and we could go home again. In previous years when we had gone north to the summer resort town of Baguio, or south to visit Auntie and Uncle Dick, we had always traveled in a first-class car with air conditioning and comfortable upholstered seats. This train was made up of third-class cars with no cooling system. The seats were as hard as wooden park benches. This journey would certainly be a new experience.

All of our fellow passengers were native Filipinos, and every one of them a different person now that the train was in motion. Smiles lighted their faces and happy talk filled the car. Some of the natives carried their belongings in woven-straw shopping bags. Others had split-bamboo baskets of various shapes and sizes. Many of the baskets now served as seats in the aisle for their owners. Those held carefully on laps probably contained lunch.

The train was moving so slowly that there was very little breeze coming in the open windows. All too often, we stopped at crossroads while lines of army trucks were allowed the right-of-way. In fact, so much time was taken up in this way that the sun was already high in the sky and heating the interior of the train to near oven-like conditions. Small children were restless and cranky.

"My goodness!" declared Mother. "It's already half past ten and we're not even out of Makati district yet." Then, pointing out the window, she added, "Look up ahead there, girls. I think that's Nichols Field. If you could see out the window on the other side, you'd see Nielson Field. There certainly is a lot of smoke around here."

Just as we thought we were really going to gain some speed, and might in fact finally leave the city outskirts behind us, the train was braked hard. People and bundles bounced around like ping-pong balls. Jolted into a sudden awareness of the train's location, an expectant silence fell over the passengers. Then in the distance we could hear the keen wailing of sirens.

"Lord help us!" cried Mother. "An air raid! Here of all places!"

There was a stampede for the door, as no one wanted to be caught on a train during a bombing. Some passengers jumped from the windows. The sirens at both military bases continued to wail as pandemonium prevailed on the train.

"I don't hear any planes or bombs yet," Mother said loudly, grabbing us each by the arm. More afraid of the panic around us, she held us back until nearly everyone else had left the car. Then we quickly jumped down to join the others running across a field toward a stand of trees.

Now we could hear the drone of high-flying planes. At that same moment, the first bombs began to explode. With our hearts beating in our throats, we ran faster. Stumbling and tripping, we reached the trees at last. Many people were lying in ditches or any other low place they could find. We cowered behind the trunk of a huge acacia tree. It was the only protection left.

Bombs were falling everywhere. Anti-aircraft guns were firing continuously. Shrapnel whined through the air as dirt and debris fell all around us. I shut my eyes tightly and held my hands cupped over my ears to hold out the deafening roar. Never had I been so frightened. I did not expect to live another minute.

I don't know how long we stayed there like that; the bombing seemed to last a lifetime. We did not leave our hiding place until we could no longer hear any guns or planes. Then, by ones and twos, people began to rise and look about them as if in a daze. Gradually the stunned passengers staggered back to the train. We followed their lead woodenly. Fortunately the train had not been strafed. The engineer was anxious to get it away from this dangerous area. He tooted his whistle to hurry the stragglers along.

Now that the immediate danger was past and we began to relax a little, we found we could not control our trembling. It was impossible to speak, for even our teeth chattered as if we were cold. Our only comfort was in each other; the three of us huddled together on one seat. And so we remained, mile after mile, recovering from a terror we had never experienced before.

"Rackety-rackety" was the sound of wheels on rails as the train, now in open country, chugged along at top speed. Rice paddies alternated with sugarcane fields. Widely scattered grass shacks led to hot, dusty little villages where people waved to our passing train. The sameness of the landscape brought a welcome heaviness to our eyelids. We drifted in and out of awareness for an hour or two.

A gradual slowing of the train, along with the increasing bustle of a few passengers gathering their things, roused us. We were just pulling into a depot. I stuck my head out the window and spied a vendor hawking sarsaparilla and some sticky-looking sweets. He and his customers bargained back and forth good-naturedly. This was a country where buyers felt honor bound to haggle the price down at least a centavo or two. Vendors, as well, felt cheated of some fun if their prices were not challenged.

"Mother, could we buy some of those little rice cakes?" I asked. "I'm getting awfully hungry." Trying to gain an ally, I nudged Carole. "Aren't you?"

"Now, Georgia, you know your father won't allow us to eat any of the native foods which we can't peel or rinse in disinfectant. We'll just have to content ourselves with the cheese sandwiches and cookies I brought."

"How about the sarsaparilla to drink?" chimed in Carole. "It's in bottles. Daddy said anything bottled is okay."

"Well, all right," agreed Mother wearily. "We do need something to drink in this heat."

So I called to the vendor and beckoned him over. With the coin Mother gave me, I bought three bottles and we had our lunch. Feeling so much better after our nap and lunch, we were almost able to push the events of the morning out of our minds. We looked forward eagerly to reaching our destination.

The hour preceding sunset found us skirting the northeastern end of Tayabas Bay. Glorious colors radiated from the setting sun and were perfectly reflected in the placid water, thereby doubling an already spectacular panorama. From there we followed the tracks south along a narrow neck of land. Darkness closed in as we turned inland and crossed over to the eastern side of the isthmus.

The train stopped at virtually every little town, and it seemed we would never reach Tagkawayan. The mine where Uncle Dick worked in 1941 was in the hills about an hour's tortuous ride by car from Tagkawayan. It was the remoteness of this mining camp that made his home sound so inviting in that perilous time. Weariness was about to overcome us as the train slowed once more. The station was unlit, and no town name could be seen. Apparently the whole village was asleep. I settled back hoping the next stop would be ours.

Just then I saw headlights coming toward us. A truck pulled up to the platform and a man jumped out. Could that be . . . ?

"That's your Uncle Dick!" Mother said excitedly. "We're finally here."

No sooner had she said that than both Uncle Dick and Auntie were beside us, everyone hugging and kissing and talking all at once.

He grabbed our bags and said with a big grin, "Follow me, ladies." He and Dad were no more alike than apples and oranges; the family name was about all they had in common. My uncle was as dark as Dad was fair, and taller too. He was a hearty, friendly man. Dad was quiet and distant.

Auntie walked Carole and me to the truck with her arms around us. As an aunt, she was absolutely the best and one of the dearest people I ever knew. A sweet and generous person, she was also striking in appearance. A slight and delicate frame was literally crowned with heavy, dark hair worn in a long braid wrapped around her head. Just above her right temple was a wide streak of white hair that was all the more noticeable for the darkness of the rest.

"In just a little while we'll have you both safe in bed," she murmured, giving my shoulder an extra squeeze.

With the bags thrown into the back of the truck, the five of us piled into the cramped cab. Our journey, which began at six in the morning and should have taken no more than eight hours, was almost over at eleven p.m.

Mother and Auntie had a lot of visiting to catch up on; they lost no time in starting. Uncle Dick's attention was wholly on the narrow, rocky trail cut through the jungle to the mine. As I watched him in the soft glow of the dashboard light, a feeling of warm, cozy security enveloped me. No harm could come to us now.

Chapter 3

Next morning I awoke to the peaceful sounds of roosters crowing and birds chirping. Pulling aside the mosquito net which surrounded my bed, I ran to the window. The mining camp was just as beautiful as I remembered.

It was spread across a narrow valley with hills rising sharply in all directions. My uncle's house and two others were on this side of the valley, about halfway up the slope. Across from us on another hill were three more houses. The mine's executives lived in these six homes, built in the native style, on stilts. Near the top of still another hill was the mine shaft. I could hear faint sounds of machinery floating down from there.

At the base of the hills was a small stream tumbling between low banks. Along both sides of the brook stood rows of small grass shacks occupied by the Filipino miners who worked here. Beyond those huts, on a narrow strip of level ground, was a badminton court. Right next to that was the company store. As far as the eye could see, jungle growth covered the hills like a dark green blanket pulled right up to the base of the mine shaft.

Our visit in this lush hideaway was a time of both tranquility and excitement, of adventurous activity and quiet rest. It was a memorable vacation in many ways. There were no other women or children at the mine; we were given the run of the entire camp. No one ever refused us a game of checkers or cards. When we brought out the badminton rackets, there was always a volunteer ready to play a game or two with us. We thoroughly enjoyed the attention. Someone brought us a pet monkey for many hours of fun and enjoyment. The monkey's name was Andres. He loved to work intently trying to remove any loose buttons from our clothing. If the threads broke, he would scamper away with the prize clutched in his tiny hand. Andres also loved peanuts and took great delight in searching our pockets for them. He would greedily stuff his cheeks so full of the little snacks that his mouth wouldn't close.

My favorite pastime was walking in the jungle looking for orchids and other wild flowers. One day Mother, Auntie, Carole, and I followed the stream away from the mining camp. We had gone into the jungle quite some distance, when we came upon a small clearing. We stood in the middle of it admiring the way sunlight streamed through the trees to form an ever-shifting pattern of light and shadow on the ground.

Suddenly we heard a noise behind us! Looking around quickly, I was startled to see a small group of people staring at us from behind a fallen tree.

When Auntie saw them she relaxed visibly and whispered, "Don't be afraid. They won't hurt us." Smiling, she offered them the bouquet of flowers she had gathered. In thoughtful silence, the natives stood their ground. Each group stared soberly at the other.

After the first few uneasy moments, I found the group fascinating. The adults, mother and father, were no taller than Carole and me. An infant sat astride its mother's hip, while a toddler clung to her hand and tried to hide behind her. Their skin was very dark brown. Their straight black hair was matted and uncombed. Neither of the children wore any clothing at all, while the adults wore only the briefest of loincloths.

Without ever coming any closer, they watched us for a few moments more and then soundlessly disappeared into the jungle.

"Who are they?" I wondered aloud.

"Pygmies," Auntie answered. "They live hereabouts in the jungle. And didn't I tell you they wouldn't hurt us?" she laughed. "They are just as curious about us as we are about them. Sometimes they come to the outskirts of the mining camp, but they never come any nearer than that. And if we try to approach them, they always leave."

Carole and I spent the rest of the day telling everyone we met about what we had seen. That adults could be the size of ten- and twelve-year-old girls proved to be a very engaging idea to us. The pygmies were quite a bit smaller than the mountain people we had seen around Baguio. The natives there, called Igorots, were of average size and wore brightly colored clothing. A chilling fact about the mountain people, though, was that they were but a generation or two removed from a history of headhunting! The pygmies, everyone assured us, were a peaceful people.

When we arrived at the mine we had no idea how long we might stay. In our optimism, we felt it would not take very long to drive the enemy from Philippine skies; probably a week or two at the most would see an end of the Japanese threat. After a couple of days, however, the war news became more and more worrisome.

The mine superintendent had a shortwave radio in his home, making it the center of our isolated community. Everyone, American and Filipino alike, acquired the habit of stopping by the house several times each day to hear the latest news. Whether the broadcasts were from Manila, San Francisco, or Darwin, Australia, the message always seemed to focus on one theme: that the line of supply to the Philippines had been wiped out when our Pacific fleet was all but destroyed at Pearl

Harbor. It might be several months before ships with ammunition, reinforcements, or even food could arrive in the Islands.

The seriousness of the war situation became very clear to me one morning after we had been at the mine only five days. A truck came roaring up in a cloud of dust to stop in front of Uncle Dick's house. An American army officer walked hurriedly up to the veranda and spoke to me. "Young lady, where can I find the manager of this mine?" he asked, wiping sweat from his forehead with a grimy handkerchief.

Attracted by the truck noise and strange voice, Auntie came to the door. Pointing across the valley, she said, "You can probably find all of the men over there at the office." Then, with concern creeping into her voice, she asked, "Is something wrong, Captain?"

"Sorry, ma'am, I'm in a hurry," replied the officer, already halfway down the steps. "I'm sure you will hear the news from the manager as soon as I leave." With that, he jumped back into the truck and drove away, hidden by yet another cloud of dust.

In spite of the hot, sunny day, a cold finger of fear traced a course along my spine, making me shiver. "Has a soldier ever come here before, Auntie?" I asked, searching my small cache of experience for a logical explanation of the captain's visit. "What do you think is the matter?" I pressed as we walked inside to the bedroom where Mother was still sewing.

"Who was that I heard you talking to, Evelyn?" Mother inquired as she rethreaded the machine.

"It was an army officer looking for the manager," Auntie replied, speaking evenly. "If the matter is of any interest to us, Porter will come tell us about it as soon as he can."

"What are you making?" I asked Mother. "Looks like a schoolbag."

Holding one up to show me, she said, "A knapsack for each of us. How do you like it?"

"It looks all right, I guess," I said half-heartedly. "But what do we need it for?"

"Well, when we go walking in the jungle we could put . . ." Her voice trailed off as we heard the front door bang shut.

"Evelyn! Dorothy! Where is everyone?" Uncle Dick's voice trailed off as he found us all gazing expectantly at the door. His first words were directed at Mother. "Are you almost finished with those?" he asked, pointing to the knapsacks.

"Just about," she answered with a quizzical look on her face.

"Good." Continuing in a very businesslike way, he added, "Here is what I want you all to do. Finish them as quickly as you can, then pack a few clothes in them for each of you: some extra socks and underwear, maybe even a sweater. Whatever you think you might need for a day or two. But save at least half of the space in each bag for food."

Auntie caught a slight pause and spoke up. "Porter, tell us what is happening. What did that man have to say?"

"Well," Uncle Dick began hesitantly. "The news is not at all good. The Japanese have landed a large invasion force at Legaspi. That isn't very far south of here."

Unable to restrain herself, Mother exclaimed, "But we came here to escape the war. Is any place safe?"

"I'm afraid this place is no longer safe," Uncle Dick told us quietly. "US Intelligence says that the enemy will soon be marching north through this area toward Manila. So Brigadier General Jones has ordered all American civilians to evacuate the province. The captain told us to have the women and children at the train depot in Tagkawayan by three o'clock this afternoon. The American army will provide you with transportation on the next military train going north. You can be back in Manila in a matter of hours. And right now Manila appears to be the safest place."

Auntie seemed so stunned by what she was hearing that she had trouble speaking. "Aren't you going with us?" she whispered.

"General Jones's orders are that nothing be left intact for the Japanese to use or otherwise benefit from." Uncle Dick spoke as casually as he could. "So all of the men will stay behind long enough to flood the mine and dismantle the machinery. Then we can leave too."

The four of us stood staring at Uncle Dick. We could not believe he was serious. Then speaking for all of us, Mother said hopefully, "I think we would all feel better if we could just wait and go with you and the other men."

"Dorothy," Uncle Dick said kindly, "if you think about it for a moment, I'm sure you will see the wisdom of you four females staying as far in front of an invading army as possible."

Mother looked at him for several seconds. When the full meaning of his words sank in, a flash of dread crossed her face and she quickly agreed. "Yes, of course, Porter. As you wish."

"I must get back to the mine now," Uncle Dick said as he edged toward the door. "But I'll be back in two hours, in plenty of time to drive you to the station." Then as an afterthought he added, "Before you start packing tell the cook to prepare a good, big meal. I don't want you starting out on empty stomachs." ·

We spent the next couple of hours hastily gathering up the few pieces of clothing we might need. It was not difficult for Mother to decide what to take because we had, after all, not brought very much with us from the city. For Auntie, however, it was a sad time; all of her earthly possessions were here in this house. She may have felt, intuitively, there was a real possibility that she might not ever see her home again or any of the things with which she had so lovingly kept house.

After a quick meal shared with Uncle Dick we climbed once again into the truck with our knapsacks piled behind the cab. For the most part, we were a silent group during that hour-long ride into the village. There was not the happy chatter between Mother and Auntie that there had been just a few days ago. Auntie sat next to Uncle Dick with her hands clasped around his arm as though trying to draw the strength from him she would soon need to say good-bye.

When we parked in front of the depot, Mother, Carole, and I got out and left them alone in the truck. We walked up and down the platform time and again. There was not another person in sight. On the spur of the moment, with no train in sight, we decided to walk the short distance into town to see if we could find the station master.

We soon came to a little *tienda* where the villagers could buy soda pop, cigarettes, and sweets. We asked the shopkeeper if he knew anything about the train or the man in charge of the depot. Unfortunately, we could neither understand him, nor he us. So, after treating ourselves to a warm sarsaparilla, we wandered leisurely back to the depot. The afternoon shadows were growing long and still no train had come. Auntie and Uncle Dick were now walking the platform.

Mother said as we approached, "Porter, it might be a good idea if you would ask the man back there at the *tienda* if he knows anything about the train. I did, but I couldn't understand any of what he said."

"Good idea. I'll be right back," he said, setting off at a trot.

In no time at all he was back, looking a little worried.

"What is it, Porter?" asked Auntie. "What did the man say?"

"Well, you know my Tagalog isn't very good," he began, "but I think he was trying to tell me that a military train went through here several hours ago. Anyway, he said there were many Americans with guns on it." Pinching his lip in thought, he added, "Sure sounded like your train."

"Oh, my goodness," Auntie murmured. "What are we going to do now?"

"Since we don't know for sure that it was your train, all we can do is wait." He was trying to sound hopeful when he continued. "Maybe that man was wrong and the train will be here soon. The captain said there would be one coming through this afternoon."

Wait we did. Through late afternoon and sunset we waited. With all hope nearly gone, we sat waiting on the platform in total darkness. There seemed nothing else to do.

Suddenly Uncle Dick jumped down and stumbled over to the tracks. "I hear something!" he exclaimed.

We all listened as hard as we could. Sure enough, there in the distance was just the faintest rumble. Whatever it was, it was coming closer.

"It's a train," shouted Uncle Dick. "I can feel the vibration on the tracks! Everybody, up on the platform. And put your knapsacks on."

Looking south, we could now see the single light on the front of the locomotive flicker off and on as it approached through the jungle trees toward us.

"Do you think it's our train, Uncle Dick?" Carole asked.

Before he could answer, Mother said as if to herself, "That might be a load of Japanese soldiers. They could have captured a train and be heading for Manila."

There was a moment's pause and then Uncle Dick said, "You might be right. Let's take cover in that grove of trees over there until we know for sure the train is in friendly hands."

So saying, he grabbed Carole and me by the hand and led the way as fast as he dared in the dark. We had no sooner reached the safety of the trees than the train screeched to a stop. We waited tensely for some sign that it was safe to show ourselves. We could hear nothing above the constant chugging of the engine.

Then a lone figure carrying a lantern swung down from the cab. He walked the length of the platform holding his light high as if looking for something. Finding nothing, he reboarded his train for departure.

At that moment Uncle Dick broke free of our little group and ran right down the middle of the tracks waving his arms and shouting, "Wait! Wait!"

The rest of us followed, almost blinded by the engine's headlight. The engineer and Uncle Dick were yelling at each other in excited voices. Both men were pointing first north and then south.

Turning to us, Uncle Dick said, "I think he's saying this is the last train going north. The Japanese seem to be advancing fast. Maybe you four ought to . . ."

"You come go me!" the agitated engineer yelled to us in broken English. "Womans go Manila!" With that, he jumped down and ran back along the train, motioning for us to follow him. He pushed a huge sliding door open and indicated we should get in.

"It's a freight train," Auntie uttered in dismay, as her voice pleaded with Uncle Dick to wait for the military train.

We all looked at him questioningly. The doubt on his face could be seen even in this dim light; should he send us north in the care of anyone except the US Army? Or should he keep us here waiting for a train that might never come? When the engineer turned away in frustration and started back toward the locomotive, my uncle acted swiftly. First he swung Carole up into the car and then me. Mother followed in the same fashion. After a brief hug Auntie was beside us in the boxcar. There was no time for lengthy farewells, so sudden was our leave-taking.

The train was already moving when Uncle Dick called, "See you in a few days."

"Porter, take care," called Auntie in a trembling voice.

If something terrible happened to Uncle Dick, we might never see him again. Maybe something terrible would happen to us traveling by ourselves through a countryside at war. Regardless of the reason for my pain, my throat was so constricted that I could not say good-bye. I waved long after Uncle Dick had faded into the darkest of night.

Chapter 4

Once again we were fleeing an as yet unseen enemy, our train rocking and clacking north through the moonless night. Huddled together, we sat on the floor of the boxcar in a corner, sometimes napping, but mostly talking to bolster our courage. Every hour or two the train stopped at small unlit depots, but no one else boarded our boxcar. We never had any desire to get off the train to stretch our legs; the fear of being left behind kept us on board.

Daylight found our train limping to a stop in a small town where only a few early risers were going about their business. The engineer came to our car and urged us in sign language to go get something to eat. We still had some canned food, but Auntie decided to follow the man into town and buy some fresh coconuts or bottled drinks for us. She soon returned with news relayed by an interpreter.

"He said the train has something wrong with its boiler," she explained. "The man who translated for me said we may have a long wait while it is fixed. He also said we could pass the time at his home, if we like."

Auntie looked doubtfully at Mother. "What do you think we should do, Dorothy?"

"Well," said Mother resolutely, "I don't think we should go to his house. We might not know when the repairs were finished on the train. If this really is the last train, we must be on it when it pulls out."

So the rest of the morning we stayed around the train, inspecting the different boxcars. We hoped to find one that would be more comfortable than the one in which we had spent the previous night. We finally decided on one that had some sacks of rice at one end. There were also some baskets of small dried fish that smelled awful, but at least if we had to spend another night on the train we could sleep on the rice sacks.

After a lunch of canned food from our knapsacks we wandered up to the head of the train to see how the workmen were progressing with repairs. When the harried foreman noticed our presence, he told us amiably, "Soon, soon." We found this friendliness and willingness to help a hallmark of all the Filipinos we met during our return to the city.

It wasn't long before the engine started chugging again, working up a head of steam. We climbed back on board, anxious to be on our way. Suddenly the train gave a lurch, throwing us all off our feet.

"Help!" yelled Carole from over by the fish baskets. "I can't get out!" All that was visible of her was a pair of legs dangling from the knees and two hands gripping the edge of a basket.

Giving her a hand out, Mother began brushing salt and bits of fish off her clothes. Carole was so chagrined that none of us had the heart to chuckle at her predicament. She was more annoyed at smelling of fish than she was hurt.

Our return trip to Manila had already passed the twenty-four-hour mark when we arrived at the outskirts of a fair-sized town. Creeping toward the depot no faster than a man could walk, the train went through a series of dragging stops and jerking starts until, with a final screech, we came to a complete standstill. With dismay, we heard the engine shut down. It looked like we would be sleeping on the rice sacks that night.

The engineer confirmed my worst fears when he said at our boxcar door, "No more go today." Carrying his lantern against the night's blackness, he led us into the station. Fortunately the station master spoke a little English. He told us that a blackout had been ordered by the American army. Our train had been in violation of that edict by traveling this far after sunset with its lights on.

Mother asked, "Is there a hotel where we can stay tonight?"

The kindly man thought for a moment and then answered apologetically, "Not good for Americans. Very dirty." But then a gleam of inspiration lit his face. "Best for you ma'ams stay here tonight."

With much apprehension, I looked around the spooky waiting room. The single lantern threw eerie shadows on the walls, and even the slightest of sounds echoed hollowly in the high-ceilinged room. The rice sacks seemed almost preferable to this lonely place.

Auntie certainly spoke for me when her soft voice broke the silence. "Oh, I don't think we should stay here by ourselves. Do you, Dorothy?"

But the man was determined to do us a favor. He dismissed our reluctance with smiling persuasiveness. "You be safe here." Patting himself on the chest, he added, "I be your guard." Our would-be benefactor must have sensed a weakening on the part of Mother and Auntie, and thought he knew just how to settle the matter. "The hotel have many fancy ladies with visitors."

That settled it. We stayed the night in the depot. Before leaving us, the train engineer helped the station master move benches around so that we could have makeshift beds close to each other. Using our knapsacks for pillows, we stretched out on what seemed almost like real beds, at first. As the night wore on, though, the benches grew harder and the mosquitoes hungrier. To make matters worse, our "guard" was sound asleep on a bench that he had pulled across the doorway. He snored unmercifully.

The second full day of our journey back to Manila was no shorter or easier than the first. It was, however, very different. As we roused from an endless night of slapping mosquitoes, the station master bustled into the waiting room, picking his teeth. Obviously an early riser, he had already eaten his breakfast.

"Good morning, ma'ams," he beamed. "Fine day today."

Tossing and turning all night long had not done much for our appearance or dispositions. Mother stood up stiffly and tried hard to appear alert and capable. "Yes," she said with an unaccustomed shortness. "Tell me, do you know when our train will be ready to leave?"

The man's smiling face quickly dissolved into sadness. "Oh, ma'am. Very sorry. Train not go north today." Wringing his hands in sympathy for our plight, he made the grave announcement, "US Army say train must go south. Get more soldiers."

We all gathered around staring at the poor man in disbelief. Carole summed up our frustration with the plaintive question, "Are we going to have to walk the rest of the way?"

Trying to be helpful, the station master said, "Maybe there be another train tomorrow."

"That won't do," Mother said brusquely. "We must go to Manila today." With a hint of panic in her voice, she added, "The Japanese are coming!"

"Yes, ma'am." The mere mention of the enemy moved the man to action. "I get help for you," he said over his shoulder as he hurried away.

"What's he going to do?" I asked, following him to the door.

"It would be hard to say," Auntie said. "But we've got to trust him. He's certainly tried to help us."

While we waited for his return, we dug through our knapsacks and found only a few crackers and a can of tomatoes for our breakfast. Before we had hardly finished the last of it, the man called excitedly from the door, "Come. Come see. This take you to San Pablo, over there." He must have been pointing somewhere, but we all had our eyes on the *carabao* and cart standing in front of us.

Moving her eyes slowly from the bulky animal to the station master, Mother asked, "How will it help us to go to San Pablo? That's still a long way from Manila."

Smiling proudly, as if he were personally responsible for the railroad schedule, he said, "That train there go north today. Maybe."

Mother and Auntie quickly put their heads together to decide how much of our money could be spent on an oxcart. While they bargained with the cart driver, Carole and I jumped up into the back and found places to sit among the sacks of coconuts and chicken coops. I had always wanted to ride in one of these two-wheeled carts, but they were used mainly in rural areas, so this was my first chance. This was going to be fun!

Auntie offered our Good Samaritan some money for all his trouble. With an embarrassed wave of his hand, he refused. "Buy some food for the girls. Not to worry about the Japanese. Soon they all gone." For emphasis, he drew a finger across his throat and made a horrible gurgling noise to indicate the quick death about to overtake the enemy. It fairly made the back of my neck crawl.

By now, a small group of townsfolk was gathered around the cart to watch us. Smiling and pointing, they seemed to find our situation very interesting. I found it a little embarrassing. Why couldn't we start? Wasn't there some danger of missing the train in San Pablo?

"Thank you very much for your kind help," Mother said to the station master.

With those parting words, she and Auntie climbed up into the driver's seat and everyone waved good-bye. At the last moment, an elderly woman in the crowd handed Auntie her own hat. Much to the amusement of the crowd, Auntie put it on and called a grateful "thank you."

Seated on the bare back of his native ox, our driver flicked a switch several times over the animal's rump and shouted excitedly at it. Only mildly aware of all the ruckus, the reluctant *carabao* lumbered into motion and began to plod lazily down the dirt road. At this pace it would take a whole week to reach San Pablo.

It took less than an hour's ride in the primitive conveyance to convince the four of us of one thing: if we ever arrived at San Pablo, we would never ride in a native oxcart again. The wooden wheels were covered with only a thin strip of hard rubber. There were no springs on the undercarriage, so the going was extremely rough. Bumping and swaying along the rutted road became an excruciating ordeal. We clung to the sides of the cart for dear life.

To add to our misery, the sun climbed ever higher in the sky and grew so hot that heat waves shimmered on the horizon. In one village we passed through, some people gave us each a banana leaf to shield us from the tropical sun.

Farther on, some field workers were having their noon meal. They readily agreed to exchange some of their food for one of our knapsacks and my hairbrush. The boiled rice and crispy pieces of fried pork served on a banana leaf were delicious. We ate greedily. Neither Mother nor Auntie mentioned anything about native food being unclean. Our hunger today was more immediate than a possible case of dysentery tomorrow. Full and content for the moment, we left the group of farmers to their siesta.

Returning to our torture-chamber-on-wheels, we plodded on. We learned that plodding and wallowing is what *carabaos* do best. They love nothing better than a long soak in muddy water. Consequently our driver had a lot of trouble keeping his animal on the road whenever we passed a pond or stream. This beast, like all others of his breed, could not be hurried in the heat of day; our progress was vexingly slow.

About midafternoon we begged our driver for a brief rest. He obliged us in the shade of a rubber tree. While we stretched our legs, he rummaged through the produce in the cart, looking for something. Suddenly he was approaching us with an eighteen-inch knife. That gave me a scary moment before I realized he was also carrying several green coconuts. Dumping them on the ground at our feet, he proceeded to husk one after another with the knife. After he deftly poked out the eyes, he handed one to each of us. We didn't have to be told to drink. The milk was deliciously refreshing. Then the cracked nuts provided us with fresh coconut to eat.

Upon reaching San Pablo, our progress through the streets was heralded by some young boys running alongside our cart yelling, "Americanas! Americanas!"

At the station we bought four tickets, which left us with very little money. With the train leaving soon, we would be in Manila before dark. But any hopes of ending our two-day odyssey did not take the wartime train schedules into account. The sun was lowering in the west before we pulled out of the station. Comfortably seated in the second-class coach, we happily watched the scenery move past our open window.

It soon became apparent that we would be making a stop at every little town. In each one a few people with tickets boarded our coach, but even more people climbed on top of the cars. Philippine custom allowed those natives who did not have the fare to ride in this manner. Since this particular train had no freight cars, the farmers were able to keep an eye on their baskets of produce while riding free to the big city market.

"This train can't pass even a *nipa* shack without stopping," exclaimed Carole crossly.

"Must be a lot of people fleeing the enemy just as we are," soothed Auntie.

"Or farmers trying to sell what they can in the city before the invaders confiscate everything," spoke up Mother.

"When there isn't room for one single more person or bundle, we won't have to stop anymore," I said logically.

After a time, the train looked and smelled like a moveable market. Crates of live chickens and ducks and several heavy baskets, each containing a small squealing pig, perched on top of our car. There were even a few cages of loudly scolding monkeys handed up to join the growing pile. Added to all that were the inevitable sacks of native sweet potatoes, coconuts, and bananas.

Darkness was settling over the waters of Laguna de Bay when we pulled into Los Banos. The hills above the far shore of the lake were covered in deep blue shadow. At the depot we sat waiting for the train to continue toward Manila. But then the engine was shut down and people began getting off.

"I wonder what the problem is now," said Auntie, looking out the window.

"I just wish we could go home," grumbled Carole. She sounded as tired as I felt.

A railroad official came to our window and explained that it would be necessary for us to spend the night in Los Banos. According to the telegraph, there was an air raid in progress around Manila. The blackout dictated no traveling with lights, and the railroad forbid traveling without them. So we were stuck for another night.

"If you will come with me, I will take you to a hotel nearby where you can sleep tonight," the man told us in perfect English.

So we followed him through the crowd of noisy passengers, aided only by a flashlight covered with a dark cloth. At the hotel, he was able to secure a cheap room for us. Still, it took the last of our money.

With the door locked behind us and the window shutters pulled to hide the lighted candle given us, we surveyed our lodging. Two narrow beds with mosquito nets nearly filled the small room. The mattresses were thin and hard, but at least we would not have to fight mosquitoes all night long. Too tired to realize that we had not eaten since the middle of the afternoon, we went to bed with our clothes on. But rest did not come to us that night.

I awoke to the sensation of a burning itch all over my body. I shook Auntie next to me and whispered, "Is there anything biting you?"

"What, dear?" she mumbled, scratching her arm.

"Something is chewing me to pieces!" I said, louder.

"There's something biting me too," Mother said from the other bed. "I'm going to have a look." Jumping up, she lit the candle and carefully checked both nets for mosquitoes.

"There aren't any inside the nets," she said, unable to understand what was causing the problem.

Carole, asleep until now, rolled over and asked sleepily, "What's the matter?"

At that moment Mother saw a little bug crawling on Carole's neck. "Hold still, Sis!" she said as she picked it off and inspected it, while Auntie held the candle.

"Ohhhh, Dorothy!" Auntie shuddered. "It's a bedbug!"

"These beds must be full of the little demons, the way we are all scratching," Mother said in disgust.

We were utterly miserable the rest of the night. When we slept at all, it was only briefly. We scratched endlessly. The first faint hint of day found us hurrying away from the filthy place. As we neared the railroad station, we could hear sounds of activity. Most of the passengers had spent the night in, or near, the train. People everywhere were rising to stretch and straighten their clothes. The family who had occupied our seats overnight gave them up readily when we approached. Once again we sat ready and waiting for the train to resume the final leg of our journey.

Two hours drug by and we were no closer to home than we had been the night before. A food vendor came on the train, selling to an eager crowd. Mother and Auntie had a little difficulty coaxing him to take some of our personal things instead of money. He reluctantly decided to take all of our toothbrushes and the toothpaste and one of Auntie's blouses. In return, we each got a small leaf-wrapped bundle of hot rice and a bottle of cream soda. We also got a large rice-flour pastry to divide amongst us.

We mimicked our fellow passengers by eating from the rice bundles with our fingers. The pastry—a delicious, thick pancake-like creation, sprinkled with brown sugar and freshly grated coconut—we tore into pieces. The food was filling and made up for no supper the previous night.

Our long wait finally ended about midmorning. Loaded to the rooftop, the train began to move ponderously north. It made no stops. The closer we came to the place where we had been bombed the week before, the more nervous Mother became. But the bombers must have gone somewhere else that day, because there was no air raid as we entered the city limits. At last we reached Tutuban Station and hailed a horse-drawn carriage to take us home.

Clip-clopping down nearly deserted streets, I could hardly believe my eyes; Manila had changed so much in our absence. Windows everywhere were broken.

Stores were closed. Piles of rubble were here and there. I could see gaping holes where once buildings had stood. The pungent smell of smoke hung heavily in the air. Most noticeable of all, there were hardly any people on the streets. It was a shocking scene.

Mother told the driver to wait for his fare as he halted his horse in front of our building. Numb with shock and fatigue, we got down stiffly and slowly climbed the stairs to our apartment. A weak knock on the locked door was all Mother could manage.

Dad opened the door and stepped back in surprise. He looked at us doubtfully, unable to accept the reality. As dirty as street urchins and with faces red and swollen from insect bites, we must have presented a dreadful sight.

"Dorothy?" he breathed, still disbelieving.

Chapter 5

"Three days," Mother sighed, leaning against the door. "And I didn't have enough money to pay the carriage driver."

Looking around us, Dad inquired, "Where's Porter?"

"He had to stay behind to close down the mine," Auntie told him. "But he should be here in a day or two."

While they were talking at the door, Carole and I slipped past them into the living room and sprawled on the sofa. I was so glad to be home. I looked around as if really seeing the room for the first time. Finding all the familiar things in the same old places was very reassuring to me. Maybe the world as I knew it had not completely disappeared.

"Girls!" Mother had caught sight of us. "Don't sit on or touch anything. There may still be bedbugs on us!"

We jumped up as though prodded from behind. We didn't want those horrible pests in our house either.

"Straight to the shower, everybody," ordered Dad. "Put all your clothes in a pile at the door, and I'll burn them right away. I'll go pay the driver too."

Once cleaned up and fed, we told Dad about our trip home. In happier times, Dad was not often given to showing his emotions, but now he looked as though he could hardly believe what he was hearing. He asked a few questions, but for the most part, Mother and Auntie needed no encouragement. They told our saga at great length. Carole and I chimed in occasionally with tidbits and details as seen from our vantage point.

"So here we are," Mother concluded.

Dad gazed at each of us in turn with a mixture of approval and pride. He was very pleased that Mother and Auntie had managed so capably what had been a difficult and trying journey. Carole and I were praised for our conduct as grown-up young ladies. I suppose the thought of all the mishaps that could have befallen four women traveling unprotected through a country at war had brought Dad's feelings to the surface.

"Dad, don't you think we ought to call and tell Lola and Grandpa Jake that we're home again?" I asked. "Or maybe we could go over to see them." I was anxious to touch base with my grandparents; that would have been the natural thing to do in normal times.

"I'll call them pretty soon, but right now I want you to come see what I have been doing while you were gone," Dad said, leading the way out the back door and down the stairs.

Underneath the open set of back steps, it looked as if a giant mole had been working in the dirt. "I've been digging an air raid shelter for myself," Dad said. "But now I can see it will have to be enlarged."

"Do you think it's deep enough yet?" asked Mother.

"It's not as deep as I would like for it to be, but I don't think I can go much lower without water seeping in."

"Will it be safer than staying in the bathroom?" Carole wondered.

"It certainly will," Dad answered. "When I'm finished digging, I'll pile sandbags all around it and then put a wooden roof over it with more sandbags on top of that. We'll be almost as safe as if we were in Malinta Tunnel on Corregidor."

"Has there been a lot of bombing here since we left?" I asked.

"Yes. There have been air raids almost every day and night," Dad grunted between shovels of dirt. "Most of the time, though, the bombings occur over military targets around the city."

"We heard about the terrible attack on Cavite several days ago," Auntie said. "Was it really as bad as it sounded?"

Dad tossed another shovelful of dirt and leaned on the handle. "It was very bad. The final count of dead was 1,600; that's American and Filipino, military and civilian. If only the navy had evacuated the civilians from around the base, the toll would have been much lower."

"Oh, my!" exclaimed Auntie sadly. She had held a clerical position at the naval base prior to her marriage, and now realized that some of her friends and acquaintances might have been among the casualties.

As I listened to the talk of bombings and casualties, I could feel my secret wish begin to recede from my heart like a glacier in summer. I had made a wish the day we left Manila, that when I returned life would again be as it was in pre–Pearl Harbor days: the peaceful, contented life I had known for eight years in the Philippines. Now the likelihood of that wish coming true seemed so remote as to be nearly impossible.

Almost every day began with the sound of sirens announcing either the end of last night's air raid or the beginning of the new day's raid. Our every waking moment was filled with plans and activities designed to assure our survival. Without really being aware of it, we learned to cope with the stresses of living in the midst of war.

Attempts at conducting business on a daily basis had been abandoned at Dad's insurance company. Instead of reporting for work, he spent most of his time either at home improving our air raid shelter or searching the city, between raids, for food and other useful materials. We nicknamed him "The Scrounger."

One day Dad came back from one of his forays with a whole bolt of a heavy, dark cloth. Mother and Auntie set to work making blackout curtains for all of the windows in our apartment. Carole and I helped by pinning in the hems. When they were hung, we could use lights in the evening without violating the blackout order.

Many times Dad brought home boxes of canned food from stores or warehouses that had suffered bomb damage. Looting was widespread in the city, but the authorities tended to look the other way unless there was fighting over the merchandise.

Mother kept meals prepared ahead so that we could grab a bowl or basket of food as we ran to the shelter. Two large jugs of drinking water always stood by the back door; it was Carole's job to take one, and mine, the other.

During daytime raids we sat cramped together in our sandbagged shelter. The hours there could be long and tedious, so we passed the time by playing card games or reading. When the air raid siren wailed at night, we spread blankets on the bathroom floor; there we sang or played guessing games in the dark before going to sleep. Only if the bombs seemed to be falling close did we go to the shelter at night.

Three days after returning to Manila, during a lull in the raids, Carole and I were sitting on the front steps. Julio, the boy from my class who lived in the big house next door, came over to talk.

"There has been no school since you left," he told us in his familiar Spanish accent. Scowling in displeasure, he continued, "That was okay for a few days, but now I am tired of nothing to do."

"Well, Dad wouldn't let us go if school did reopen," I said, not looking up from the scarf I was knitting. Before the war, the Red Cross had enlisted all the girls at school who knew how to knit to make scarves for the Allied soldiers in Europe. "He won't let us leave home as long as there are air raids."

"Look," said Carole, pointing down the street. "I wonder who that is."

After a quick glance, Julio muttered, "Doesn't look like anyone who lives around here."

"Georgia, look!" Carole shook me impatiently. "You can stop knitting long enough to look one second."

My eyes moved unwillingly down the block until they lit on a tall, thin man walking slowly toward us. He was carrying a bag in each hand and was hunched over a little bit. There was a knapsack on his back.

"Could it be Uncle Dick?" I whispered doubtfully, watching closely. In an instant of recognition, I gasped, "It is Uncle Dick! Go get Auntie!" Unmindful of my knitting, which fell in the dirt, I raced down the street, my feet hardly touching the sidewalk.

Falling in to walk beside him, I asked eagerly, "Can I carry something for you?" He looked so tired. I wondered how anyone that tired could still put one foot in front of another.

"No thank you, Georgia." He managed a weak smile. "My load is balanced, and I must not stop until I can lay it all down."

By now Auntie was running toward us with Carole skipping along beside her. When Auntie was close enough to see him well, she stopped in horror and exclaimed, "Porter, my dear! Let me help you."

"Auntie, he said he can't stop until he gets inside the house," I explained, taking her hand. "I think he's even too tired to talk very much."

Fortunately, Dad and Mother met us at the front steps. Dad insisted that he carry the bags upstairs. "What have you got in them?" grunted Dad as he took one from his weary brother.

"Gold bullion," mumbled Uncle Dick.

Auntie helped him remove the knapsack from his back and told us, "You girls can carry that up between you."

With his arms draped over Auntie's and Mother's shoulders, Uncle Dick was just barely able to stumble up the stairs. We staggered under our loads, making quite a lot of noise in the hall. Some of our neighbors opened their doors just wide enough to peek out, closing them again just as quickly.

Suffering from complete exhaustion, Uncle Dick had to be helped to bed. He fell asleep immediately and slept until the next morning. His sleep could not have been very restful, as he tossed and turned all night. He muttered often, even yelled a couple of times. His trip to Manila must have been long and hazardous to cause him such nightmares. Neither Auntie nor anyone else in the house slept much that night.

The next day, while we sat through another air raid in the shelter, Uncle Dick told us about his journey to the city with the gold bricks.

He and the other men left the mine in a truck three days after we did. They went as far as Altimonan before gas became impossible to buy. The US Army had appropriated all available supplies, so they abandoned the truck and hired native oxcarts. In this painfully slow manner they reached Lucena.

"Is your fanny sore like ours were from riding in that cart?" I asked, making a wry face.

"What makes you think so?" he joked. "Aren't oxcarts as comfy as your Grandpa Jake's Studebaker limousine?"

On the second day, the men switched to the railroad, reaching Santa Rosa in a boxcar before being forced off by military order. General Jones and his army units were blowing up railroad tracks and bridges leading to Manila.

"Did the bedbugs bite you in that hotel in Los Banos?" asked Carole, showing him the bites on her arms and legs.

"I didn't stay in a hotel either night. What little rest I got was on railroad station benches."

"How did you come up from Santa Rosa?" Dad urged him to continue his story.

"At Santa Rosa, we thought the best way to proceed was by canoe across Laguna de Bay. Because of the precious loads we carried, we split up and rented a canoe for each of us. I haven't seen any of the other men since then." He shook his head worriedly, remaining silent for a while.

"Why? What happened to the other men?" My question broke the silence.

"Well, it was early afternoon when we started north across the water. The four boats were able to stay together for a time. But then the wind came up, and the water got choppy; distances between the boats began to widen. By late evening I couldn't see any of the other boats in the gloom."

"Porter, how much sleep did you get during this time?" asked Auntie, studying the worn face she loved so dearly.

"That first night in Lucena, when we were still together, the four of us took turns standing guard over the gold while the others slept. But by myself last night, I didn't dare fall asleep. My boatman put me ashore near Pasay. I walked into the village and sat up all night in the depot. From Pasay I rode the bus to the corner down there on Taft Avenue and walked here." His story told, Uncle Dick reached for the jug of water and drank thirstily.

Dad cleared his throat and commented solemnly, "I would venture to say your greatest danger was more from brigands and thieves than the Japanese along the way."

"Men have been killed for much less gold than I carried," Uncle Dick agreed. "The four of us brought out all there was at the mine. A fortune!"

Auntie took her husband's hand in her own and said huskily, "Let's be thankful we are all here safe and sound now." Her eyes glistened with happy tears.

After the all-clear signal sounded later that day, the brothers took the bullion to the mine company's bank downtown. His responsibility to his employer then over, Uncle Dick signed up at the US Army motor pool and drove supply trucks for the military the remainder of December.

Two days before Christmas, the entire Barnes family went to visit Lola and Grandpa Jake Rosenthal. Being Dad's mother, she was of course my grandmother, but we were never allowed to call her by any of the conventional names used for such a relative. She was simply Lola, though that was not her given name. Lola was a generous grandmother, but an exacting one. She was very strict about good manners.

Grandpa Jake, Lola's second husband, was not my real grandfather, though you would never have guessed it from the warmth of our relationship. He was a very dear old man, and Carole and I both adored him. His hair was white and silky, his waistline rotund; a flowing beard was all he lacked to complete the Santa Claus image. He was fun to visit because he gave every indication he enjoyed our company.

During the last few months, Grandpa Jake had suffered from a serious heart problem and was often confined to bed. When we entered his sickroom that day, he looked especially pale and weak. Jose, his Filipino valet, stepped away from his post at the bedside, so we could go closer.

"Well now, look who's come to see me." Grandpa Jake reached out to take our extended hands in his. "My favorite gold-diggers of '49."

"Grandpa Jake, why do you always call us that?" exclaimed Carole in a mock scolding voice. Part of the ritual was protesting the name and insisting on a reason for it. Grandpa Jake always declined to explain, but I think I understand it now; he meant we would be of marriageable age, eighteen and twenty, by the year 1949 and would therefore be looking for rich husbands.

Lola allowed us only a few minutes to stay at his bedside. Grandpa Jake was apparently much sicker than we realized. "Come, girls, let him rest for a while."

The rest of our brief visit was spent in the large living room of their old Spanish-style home. Lola presided over a family discussion that really included only her sons. Mother and Auntie were not expected to comment unless asked to do so. Carole and I could only listen. Lola was a matriarch of the old school.

The family meeting concerned the physical condition of Grandpa Jake. He was too sick to go to and from an air raid shelter several times a day, and yet it was really unsafe for them to remain in the house. If the raids grew any worse, well . . . what then? Wouldn't it be wise to put him in a hospital? The enemy would not bomb a building clearly marked with a red cross, would they? And so the talk went.

The final decision was to wait a few more days. Perhaps then it would be clearer which direction the war was going. Even though the Japanese army was closing in on the city of Manila from all directions, we continued to hope, unrealistically, for a miracle.

On Christmas Eve, Uncle Dick came home after a long day at the motor pool. He seemed more depressed and worried than tired. "A rumor I heard frequently today was that General MacArthur and his staff have moved their headquarters out to the island of Corregidor," he said despondently. "He has abandoned us all to the enemy."

"That fits in with what I heard." Dad's voice was heavy with concern. "President Quezon, his family and cabinet have also gone to Corregidor."

"Have we lost the war, Dad?" I asked.

"Not quite," he reassured me quickly. "General Wainwright is gathering all the USAFFE men for a stand on Bataan. If they can hold out until President Roosevelt sends reinforcements, we may still beat the Japanese."

"I'm afraid they won't arrive in time," declared Uncle Dick quietly. "The Philippines are lost already."

"You may be right," replied Dad with resignation. "We'll know in a few days."

That night we had our Christmas celebration. We had been under almost constant air raid alert for the last twenty-four hours, but the all-clear sounded just before sunset. It was decided to go ahead with our festivities right away, before the usual night raid began.

To be near the back stairs and shelter, just in case, Carole and I set our coffee table in the kitchen and spread it with a white cloth. Sofa cushions on the floor would serve as seats. In the center of the table, Mother placed a single candle. Auntie had stripped a small tree branch of its leaves, planted it in a can of dirt, and hung a few decorations on it. That was our Christmas tree.

To the sound of interminable explosions both near and far, we sat down to eat our holiday meal. Fires around the city cast a dim glow through our blackout curtains, thus painting our walls a strange shade of purple. The meal must have been a very ordinary one, because I don't remember what we had. More importantly, we were together and having fun.

There were gifts under the tree; we had searched through closets and drawers to find unused, forgotten items we could wrap for someone else. The six of us were almost able to drown out the sounds of war by singing Christmas carols. We even made some taffy, but it was a complete flop; it stuck to everything. Christmas 1941 was one we would look back on with fondness and yearning for several years to come.

After Christmas our world began to crumble at an alarming rate. On December 27, Manila was declared an open city. It was hoped that this move would save the city from further destruction or loss of life. The bombings, however, did not stop. With no defense left, the city lay helpless beneath the Japanese pilots who ruled the sky.

Every day the news grew grimmer. General Wainwright's forces had no real chance against the overwhelming odds they faced. Their last main objective was to hold open a narrow passage into the Bataan peninsula to enable their USAFFE comrades from southern Luzon to reach them before the Japanese could cut them off. Together on Bataan, it was hoped they could hold the enemy off for at least six months.

The Japanese, ever since landing their main force at Lingayen Gulf on December 22, had moved relentlessly southward. Their target was Manila. By December 28, they had taken Cabanatuan. In three more days they passed through Tarlac and were within thirty miles of Manila. Their arrival in the capital was imminent.

New Year's Eve 1941 was like a night at the edge of hell. For days past, hundreds of thousands of gallons of gasoline burned. Military equipment, which could not be transported to Bataan, was being destroyed. American demolition squads continued to blow up everything not meant to fall into enemy hands. A powdery ash, which covered everything like a shroud, rained down from the black umbrella of smoke.

On New Year's Day the radio warned American and other Allied nationalities to stay indoors. We were told the Japanese could enter the city at any time. The local authorities repeatedly advised against resisting the invaders.

On January 2, we stood on our back porch looking east toward Taft Avenue a block away. Between the buildings and trees we could catch just a glimpse of rank after rank of Japanese soldiers marching victoriously up that main boulevard. Not a shot was fired. Too numb to understand the implications for our future, we continued to watch until the entire column had passed our vantage point.

"What will become of us now?" Mother asked in a strangled voice. There was a hint of tears in her voice, but she did not cry. Instead, she turned and walked woodenly back into the kitchen.

On January 4, we were sitting in the living room trying to find a newscast on the radio. Suddenly there was a sharp knock at our door. My heart jumped into my mouth. Dad slowly rose from his chair and went to the door.

The opened door revealed a Japanese officer wearing a long, curved sword at his belt. Two aides stood behind him. When they bowed politely, with great ceremony, I thought the sword would poke one aide in the face. I started to giggle. Mother quickly grabbed me and pulled me to her. Her fear of them was instantly clear to me, and very sobering.

Dad was told to have his family ready in one hour; we would be picked up and taken somewhere for registration. In the meantime we should pack enough food and clothing for three days. The implication was that we would be allowed to return home in three days. Exactly one hour later we were assembled with many others from our building on the sidewalk. The Japanese ordered us, stunned with disbelief, into a truck too small for so many people and their bags.

There was no one on the empty street to witness our capture. Then I noticed Julio watching us from his bedroom window. I raised my arm, hoping my friend would wave to me, but someone pulled him away, and the curtain fell.

Chapter 6

Just a few minutes' drive from our home, the truck stopped in front of Rizal Stadium. Carrying our bags, we filed past the guards at the gate onto the playing field. The stadium, usually the scene of hotly contested soccer games, was host this day to a confused crowd milling about aimlessly.

"Where do we go to register?" wondered Dad aloud.

Apparently not hearing him, Uncle Dick remarked, "If we could get this registration business over with, maybe we could go home."

A stranger, overhearing the brothers, spoke up. "You might just as well sit down and get comfortable. My family and I have been here for hours, and we haven't yet been told what to do."

"What do you think they are going to do with us?" asked Dad. "The officers and men at the gate were awfully disorganized. No one seems to be in charge."

The stranger came closer and lowered his voice. "I've heard a rumor that we are to be taken someplace else. But nobody knows where yet." He shrugged his shoulders. "Or when, for that matter."

Not knowing whether that rumor was good news or not, we joined the wandering crowd in the hope of finding someone who knew more. After walking around for about an hour, and not learning anything further, we gave up and sat down to rest. All the while, more and more people were coming in.

"Dad, how much longer do you think we'll have to wait here?" I asked. "It'll soon be suppertime."

"I don't know, Georgia," he answered wearily. "But I'm beginning to suspect we are going to spend the night here."

The afternoon dragged on and on. Bewildered people dealt with the untenable situation in an unremarkable way: babies cried, mothers fretted, siblings argued, and family men grouped together in endless discussions of their current predicament.

Suddenly in late afternoon, the Japanese went into action. Their guttural commands, in an incomprehensible language, failed to elicit the desired response, so they grabbed some people and propelled them toward the exits where they forced them into lines. Once we understood what they wanted us to do, everyone complied readily. If the registration was not to be at Rizal Stadium, at least it looked to us as though we would be going to a place where we could be registered.

This time it was a bus our family boarded. Ours being the first to leave, we led a convoy of trucks and buses north through town to the Pasig River, and across on Quezon Boulevard. Turning east on Calle Espana, it was not long before we drove through an ornate wrought-iron gate into lovely landscaped grounds.

"What is this place, Dad?" I asked, enjoying the beauty of the extensive flower beds and blooming shrubs. "I don't think I have ever been here before."

"It's the University of Santo Tomas; started by Spanish Dominican friars back in the 1600s, it is probably over three hundred years old." Dad rambled on casually. "Of course, these buildings aren't that old. The university moved into this new campus not more than fifteen years ago."

Our convoy stopped in front of a four-story building that loomed over the wide plaza; it was clearly the administration center. A small contingent of Japanese guards, under the command of a single officer, stood at the main entrance. People began spilling out of the vehicles onto the plaza. We did not wander far before the officer began issuing orders through an interpreter.

He told us that women were to occupy rooms on the second floor of this building, while men would sleep in the gym, across campus to the southwest. Dad and Uncle Dick led us upstairs, where they decided we should be in the large room on the southwest corner. The room had windows on two sides and would be more comfortable with a circulating breeze. That would be important if we had to stay a day or two. We were still thinking in terms of a temporary stay.

Previously a classroom, it was filled with student chairs. The walls must have been between twelve and fifteen feet high and were hung with huge, elaborately framed pictures. Other women were coming into the room, so we quickly claimed one corner close to a window and proceeded to make ourselves as comfortable as possible. We pushed the chairs to one side and took the largest pictures off the walls. Stacked two or three high, they would serve as makeshift beds and keep us off the hard terrazzo floor.

Auntie looked a little concerned at first when she saw that her bed was a portrait of John the Baptist. "Let's turn it over so I can't see it," she pleaded. Then chuckling, she said, "Never mind. He would understand."

While Dad and Uncle Dick went to the gym to stake a claim there for themselves, we became acquainted with the other women in the room. Everyone had a story to tell about where they were when they first heard about Pearl Harbor, or how bad the bombings were where they lived. There were as many opinions on how long we would be held here as there were people in the room.

The next day our room filled up completely with about thirty or thirty-five women. The Red Cross served coffee for breakfast, giving us a hot drink to go with the canned goods we had packed. There was no lunch served, but the Red Cross made soup and bread available for supper.

By the end of the week we realized we were going to be in Santo Tomas longer than our captors had led us to believe. My own feelings were in a turmoil. It was unsettling to be a prisoner, especially when I didn't understand exactly what that would mean in the near or distant future. It would be days before my anxiety subsided, and then only after a semblance of order entered my life.

A routine developed in camp: up early to hurry down the hall to the bathroom, I took my place in the waiting line; then out to a small building on the plaza where the Red Cross served the entire camp. There too, I stood in line. The rest of the day was usually spent watching for the trucks that brought new arrivals every day. Friends and neighbors always brought rumors, which passed for news from the outside world. In late afternoon it was time to line up again for a supper of soup or stew.

Sometime during that first week one of Dad's friends told him that native servants were bringing packages of food to camp for their interned employers. From then on Dad or Uncle Dick hung around the front gate several hours each day hoping to see someone they knew. The ritual of waiting in the "package line," as it soon came to be known, became an important part of every day. Even those people who had no one on the outside gathered with the others because that was a good place for friends to visit and swap rumors.

After five days, our supply of canned goods was seriously depleted. Our trips to the main gate became more urgent. The day Dad came running into our room with a basket was a very important day.

"Jose!" Dad gasped, nearly out of breath. "Jose was at the gate." Without another word, he set the basket on the floor. We watched excitedly as Mother unpacked it.

"Oh, a pomelo!" Carole exclaimed, reaching for the native grapefruit. There was cooked rice and fried chicken and bananas. We began to eat immediately.

"What's this under the chicken?" asked Auntie as she pulled out a piece of waxed paper. Unfolding it, she discovered a small folded piece of stationary. "It's a note from your mother, Porter," she exclaimed, handing it to him. "Read it aloud so we can all hear."

Leaning back against the wall, he began to read in a quiet voice. "'Dear loved ones: Our home was commandeered by a Japanese officer, so we had to leave with only a couple of hours to pack what we needed. Fortunately you left a key to your apartment with me, so we came here.'"

"How is Grandpa Jake?" I broke in.

"Be patient, dear," Uncle Dick winked at me. "I'm coming to that."

"'Jake rapidly grew worse, and so I appealed to some of our well-placed Filipino friends. Mrs. Vargas was able to get permission for him to go to Philippine General Hospital, where he is being well cared for. It seems I will be allowed to stay here for the time being.

"'Jose will come to the camp every day,'" continued Uncle Dick, "'and bring as much as he can. You can send your laundry and we will return it clean. Try to send a note as often as possible to let me know what you need. I will do my best to see you get it. I have plenty of help; your servants did not leave their posts, and Jose came with me from the big house.'"

"I think we should ask for some bedding," spoke up Mother. "And we really need more clothing."

"Wait a minute," Uncle Dick laughed. "I'm not through yet."

"Whatever I send you," the letter went on, "be sure to inspect it carefully for notes and money. If I think it's safe, I'll send some of the latter for emergencies. Be careful and stay well. All my love. Mother."

Beginning with that basket, our lot improved a great deal, though it did so very slowly. In two days we had a pillow. After that came a sheet, then a second one. Each basket was filled with cooked food ready to eat. We asked for blankets and mosquito nets, clothes, shoes, books, cards, paper, and pencils. Lola became an expert at putting more in a basket than you would think possible. There was always some money. It must have been quite a chore for Jose to carry those packages. After a few days I had been all over the camp and had seen everything inside the walls. I knew in which rooms my friends were staying, where sweethearts went for a stolen kiss, and where to find a shady place on the lawn to spend a quiet hour with a book. One day while roaming the ground floor of our building, I came to a small room where a child was screaming incessantly. I paused at the door to see what was happening.

The room was a first-aid station with a nurse and a little boy sitting on his mother's lap.

"Young lady, will you come hold some of this for me?" the nurse asked, handing a roll of gauze and a pair of scissors to me. "The way this boy is squirming, I need an extra pair of hands."

I helped the nurse, Miss Davis, treat the child's cut knee and several other patients with minor hurts. It was fun. I enjoyed learning many of the things necessary for running a small clinic: cutting tape into narrow strips, rolling bandages, and whatever else I was asked to do.

"Let me guess," teased Miss Davis. "You want to be a nurse when you grow up?"

"Yes, I do." I smiled in embarrassment. I had never told anyone my secret ambition, but this friendly woman knew right away! I thought she was very clever. "Do you think I could?" I asked timidly.

"Well," she said heartily, "why don't we find out if you really like the work? Suppose you come help me every afternoon, and I'll let you try your hand at it."

"Really?" I grinned. When she nodded, all I could say was, "I'll be back tomorrow," as I went rushing off to tell Mother the exciting news.

For many weeks I helped in that first-aid station. Of course there were other nurses, and a doctor as well, but they never acted as though I was in the way. In fact, they showed me how to wrap a sprained ankle, swab cuts and scrapes, and fix a sling. The kindly staff went a long way toward making one young girl feel needed and important.

Besides doctors and nurses, the internee population in our camp, growing at a rapid rate, included a cross-section of Manila's prewar inhabitants. There were lawyers, businessmen from every field of endeavor, missionaries, and many others, as well as teachers.

Teachers from the American and Bordner Schools got together and decided that enough time had already been wasted away from classwork. Preparations to reopen school began right away. The result was a school very different from any the students had ever attended. Classes were held outside on the shady side of the Education Building from 9:30 until 12:30, six days a week. Enough seats were scrounged from around camp to accommodate the more than four hundred students. Textbooks, paper, and pencils, however, were in short supply, which meant that a major portion of our learning consisted of memorizing what the teacher put on the blackboard. In spite of these handicaps, the curriculum was limited more by the restrictions that the Japanese imposed on it. They forbade the study of current affairs, history, and geography.

For all the grumbling the students did about having to go back to school, it did give us something to do with our mornings; something much more constructive than what we had been doing. For several weeks, dozens of us kids had gathered in the far northwest corner of the camp and fought a war of our own. I'm not sure why we did it. Perhaps we were fighting back at the violence that had so recently threatened our very lives; the war had already stamped an indelible mark on our innermost beings.

Battles lasted all morning sometimes and were extremely rough. We would charge the "enemy" trench and bombard them with dirt clods, and try to prevent them from emerging from their trench to chase us off. If chased, we dueled with sticks in no-man's land. Pushing and shoving and yelling while we fought each other, we vented our fury at the world. Occasionally someone was hurt.

Returning hot and dirty from one such battle, I found Carole crying on her bed. Mother was wiping her face and arms with a wet cloth, while Auntie fussed around trying to make her comfortable. No one spoke to me.

"What's the matter with Carole?" I asked, with a sense of dread creeping over me.

"You pushed me into the ditch," moaned Carole. "And now my whole chest hurts." She looked at me accusingly, tears running across her cheeks onto the pillow.

"I did?" I murmured, knowing I was in deep trouble. "I don't remember pushing you," I defended myself.

"Did you push anyone?" Mother was very upset with me.

"Well, yes, I suppose so. It's part of the game." To Carole I said quietly, "If I pushed you, I'm sorry."

"Is that the best you can do?" Mother was really angry. "I think she may have some cracked ribs."

"Oh, really?" I gasped. "Gosh, Carole, I'm really sorry. I didn't mean to hurt you." My voice was wavering and my eyes were swimming. "I didn't even see you!"

"That's better," said Mother. "To help you remember this, you must give up your turn for the pillow so that Carole will be more comfortable." Less angry now, she added, "You are to remain in this room for the next two days except at mealtime. After that, thank goodness, school begins."

"Can't I help in the clinic anymore?" I pleaded.

"Yes, you can do that. But that's all," she said firmly. "We'll have no more of this sort of thing."

That was the end of the violent behavior for me. Once school started no one else played the war game ever again.

STIC—Santo Tomas Internment Camp—had a population of several thousand. Rooms were bursting at the seams. The Red Cross supplied canvas cots for everyone. The space allowed each person was the width of her bed plus a chair or box between hers and the next person's bed. Belongings were stored underneath the bed. In our room there were thirty-eight women and girls. Our elected room monitor was judge and jury when the inevitable disagreements arose.

Morale, not really low because no one thought this situation could possibly last, received a vitality boost toward the end of January. Among our polyglot multitude was a group of entertainers: musicians, singers, comedians, magicians, and jugglers, among others. They put on a floor show one evening that rocked the main building with applause and cheering. They poked fun at themselves and all internees as well as at our new lifestyle. It was such a huge success that it became a regular part of camp life. Even a few of the guards attended.

The Japanese, through some strange quirk in their thinking, did not feel responsible for feeding us, though they were certainly responsible for our being there. After the first two or three weeks it was no longer possible for the large number of internees to be fed from the little building used in the beginning. A much larger kitchen, still supplied entirely by the Red Cross, was installed on the ground floor at the back of the main building. It was from this facility that the entire camp would be fed until the end. Dad volunteered to be a cook.

Mother and Auntie worked on the vegetable detail each morning. They painstakingly sorted large pans of raw rice in order to remove rocks, straw, and other forms of trash. Live weevils were easy to spot because they wiggled, but the dead ones looked so much like grains of rice that it was impossible to remove them all. Rice was a staple of our diet and probably contained more protein than was normal.

The women also peeled baskets full of native sweet potatoes for boiling. Japanese guards watched the peeling detail very carefully so as to prevent the women from paring too deeply into the vegetable. The parings were as thick as the women could get by with, because they were allowed to take the parings for themselves when their work was done.

When the work was finished Carole and I and others crawled around on the ground picking up what had fallen. We added this to what Mother and Auntie had. Jose had brought us a native clay cook-stove along with some charcoal. Dad set the stove up in the main building's east patio. We often cooked ourselves something extra to eat, such as vegetable peelings. Scrubbed clean, they were boiled with a little salt, and helped fill our always-empty stomachs.

Many people had acquired native stoves. A walk through the patios any time of day would cause appetites to soar from the different aromas filling the air. Smoke filled the air too, but we didn't mind that. We had friendly arguments over what the different foods were we could smell. Everyone had an intense interest in food; that interest would increase as starvation set in.

Uncle Dick was one of the camp carpenters. They constructed the stage for our entertainment, built the dining sheds, and helped get the camp kitchen ready for business. In his spare time he made lawn chairs and wooden beds. Where the lumber came from for such projects, I can't guess, but he did very well selling the finished products. The items were either sold outright or bartered for items needed by our family. Everyone needed a lawn chair. Internees carried them everywhere: to use while waiting in line, to the floor shows, or outside to catch a breeze. The beds became increasingly popular as the Red Cross cots sagged or tore.

If there had been any doubt that we, as prisoners, were completely at the mercy of our captors, it was erased in mid-February when three men escaped over the wall at night. Their absence was discovered the next morning during roll call. Unfortunately, they were recaptured and brought back to camp shortly after noon the same day.

It was during my stint of duty at the first-aid station that we were drawn to the door by a noisy disturbance in the hall. Barely able to see through the crowd of soldiers and internees, I thought I saw a white man being pushed cruelly toward the commandant's office a few doors away. I was still peering down the hall when suddenly a Japanese guard rushed at our door. He shouted and gestured angrily. We guessed at his meaning and quickly closed the door. I was frightened half to death and had to lean against the wall to catch my breath. I looked weakly to Miss Davis for an explanation.

"It's probably the men who escaped last night," she whispered, her face pale with alarm. "If it is, I fear for their lives."

Angry words were shouted in Japanese. The unmistakable sounds of men being beaten crept under our door. Screams pierced the clinic's walls. My fear mounted to terror. The horrible din went on for what seemed like hours, until the only sound to be heard was a low, pitiful moaning.

Then we were drawn to peek out the window by the sound of a truck's engine being started. We saw the guards throw the helpless men into the back of the truck and drive away. We learned a few days later that they had been executed at the edge of a common grave. After that I understood exactly how cruel people in power could be to those at their mercy. From that day I would forever have empathy for the helpless.

Chapter 7

The months of captivity were slipping by. In anticipation of the hot season just weeks away, people began looking for a way to make life more bearable when the buildings would become too hot for comfort. Shanties seemed a good solution. With the package line working, at least for the time being, it was possible for internees to get building materials for private shanties. The Japanese imposed some rules on shanty buildings: they should be open on all sides and could be used only during daylight hours.

Shanties soon sprang up all over STIC, like mushrooms after a warm spring rain. Dad and Uncle Dick built us a small shanty on the east side of the main building. Like many others, it would have been judged squalid and tacky by prewar standards, but we thought it was cozy and wonderful. The shanty provided our family with a place to spend time together when not required to work on camp details. It had a roof made of old billboards advertising Filipino movies, which made for a colorful ceiling. On top of that was some native thatching to shed rain. The floor was dirt. It contained a table and student chairs, boxes to serve as storage for kitchen things, and our native stove.

It was here we celebrated Carole's eleventh birthday, on March 18. Since internment, it was the first real occasion for our family to celebrate. The folks made it as nice for her as they could. An adequate meal was made festive by the cake Jose brought from Lola. Carole received a few presents: a new hairbrush and barrette, and a nearly new pair of pink socks. All of these items had been acquired at the exchange store for little things the folks traded in.

As a result of the escape in February, Uncle Dick and Dad and about seven hundred other men had been moved out of the gym. It was too close to the wall. They were then housed in the Education Building, close to where our shanty was.

Now they would not have to walk that great distance in the heat and could better conserve their energy.

Shortly after Carole's birthday a series of rumors, which nearly devastated our morale, made the rounds in camps. MacArthur and his family and President Quezon and his family had all been spirited away to the safety of Australia. MacArthur left with the parting words, "I shall return." The question, "When?" went unanswered. An even harder blow to our spirits came on April 10 when we learned that the USAFFE army on Bataan had surrendered. Our morale hit bottom when Corregidor fell to the enemy on May 6. Marooned in enemy territory, we had no idea how long we would have to wait for liberation.

In time, with the acceptance of reality, STIC internees began to buckle down for the long haul. They became more careful with what little food they had; it was hoarded like gold.

Shanties were refurbished wherever practical with an eye to the rainy season coming in June. Every effort was made to acquire as much food and other necessities as possible through the package line, in the event it might someday be shut down. With hope for an early release all but dead, we endured one day at a time.

Our low spirits were raised somewhat when the main kitchen served up the first harvest from the camp garden. It was just a native spinach, but we were proud to have been able to do something toward feeding ourselves. The garden had required two long months of backbreaking work to reclaim it from an old city dump on the university grounds. The tools used were the most primitive kind. Internees, unused to manual labor in the tropics, had done the work in an exceptionally hot summer on much less than adequate rations. In view of the recent Japanese victories, the garden was seen as vital to our survival.

After lunch one day, around the middle of May, Auntie and Uncle Dick said they would wash dishes. They loaded them into a dishpan and headed for the communal wash area behind the main kitchen.

Intending to help, I was about to follow them when Dad spoke. "Stay a minute, Georgia. We have something to tell you girls."

I looked at Mother. She was smiling, so it must be good news. "Why didn't you want Auntie and Uncle Dick to hear the news?" I asked, puzzled.

"We had asked them to stay," answered Mother, "But since they already know what we are going to tell you, they felt we should have this time together, just we four."

"What is it?" asked Carole. She was excited and wanted them to get right to the point, as I did myself.

Dad cleared his throat three times! Something really important was afoot, I thought.

Finally, in a quiet voice so the people in neighboring shanties couldn't hear, Dad said, "Your mother is expecting a baby."

Carole and I sat there speechless with surprise. Could it be true? I wondered. No mention had ever been made about a possible brother or sister someday. I looked at Mother for confirmation, as if Dad were just teasing. She was beaming, obviously delighted. Well, everyone but Mother was losing weight, so it must be true. "How soon?" I asked.

"Probably around the middle of October," Mother answered. "Wouldn't it be wonderful if the baby came on the fifteenth, our wedding anniversary?"

"I don't know whether I want a brother or a sister." Carole pondered the question as if her decision could somehow make a difference.

"We really don't care which it is, do we?" I said as I went to hug Mother. "It'll be fun to hold any kind of baby."

Carole kissed Mother as I got ready to go to the clinic.

Dad interrupted these feminine proceedings with, "That's not all."

He regained our attention right away. What more could there be? We sat down again, while Dad began to talk slowly. "Because of your mother's condition, we have obtained permission for her to be released on a temporary pass. That way she can stay at the apartment with Lola until the baby is due. From there we hope she will be allowed to enter one of the city hospitals." Dad frowned as he added, "I'm afraid our camp hospital isn't the best place to have a baby."

"You mean she's going to be out there and we're going to be in here?" I exclaimed, dismayed. "We won't be able to see her for months!" How could they do this to us? We had never been separated from both of our parents at once.

"I'm coming to that," Dad replied patiently. "We were also able to have you girls released to the Holy Ghost Convent for a few months. Back in February the sisters there agreed to take in some children and a few mothers as chaperons and teachers. While you are there, Mother will be able to visit you once a week." He looked at us, perhaps hoping to see some enthusiasm on our parts for this new plan.

Carole seemed really concerned when she said, "But you won't be there either, will you, Dad?"

Dad managed a little smile. "Right now, the Japanese are letting fathers visit Holy Ghost one hour a week. I might be there once in a while when Mother is there, and then we could all be together."

"Do we have to?" I asked quietly, blindly searching for Carole's hand. It would be just the two of us now.

"Georgia," Mother said in a strained voice, "we have considered every alternative. We are certain you will be safe at Holy Ghost. We have come to the conclusion, Dad and I, that this is the only way for all of us to get the best-available care under existing conditions."

Worried more than I wanted to let on, I questioned further. "When will we be together again? Like we are now?"

"As long as the Japanese allow Mother to stay in the apartment, even after the baby comes, I think she will be better off there. But if and when she must return to camp, we will bring you girls back too." Then he added, "If we haven't been liberated before then."

Two days later, right after breakfast, Carole and I boarded a bus along with some other kids and one mother to be taken to Holy Ghost Convent. Though this was our first trip outside since January, we found the city little changed since then, except there were Japanese soldiers everywhere.

The building we entered at Holy Ghost was a white three-story stucco structure with walls extending from either side of the entrance along the sidewalk to the corners of the block. It gave the appearance of being unoccupied, so lifeless was the exterior. In fact, it was necessary to ring the bell several times before the heavy door opened slightly. A nun beckoned us in and quickly shut the door behind us.

Some female Filipino employees helped us take our things to the second floor. There we entered a large dormitory where we chose from among several empty beds. Carole would be on one side of the room, and I on the other. We were told to leave the unpacking until later because we were going directly to class. Entering a classroom, we found a catechism lesson in progress. The nun pointed toward empty chairs without missing a word about the Holy Trinity.

I knew some of the kids: two girls and one boy from Bordner, and two boys and three girls I had met in STIC. They all smiled at us; some even waved furtively. No one said a word. Bridget rolled her eyes toward the nun as if to say she was very strict about whispering in class.

Before lunch we had classes in botany and mathematics. At the sound of a bell, we all trooped down to a large dining hall on the first floor. Carole and I took our cue from the others and stood behind our chairs while a nun gave thanks for the meal. Then we could talk with our friends. We told them about the latest developments in camp and what the food was like. They told us everything they had learned about dormitory life. I began to feel better: maybe this wasn't going to be so bad after all.

After a lunch of rice and a few stewed vegetables the boys were sent to their dormitory on the third floor, and we went to ours for siesta hour. Later in the afternoon we had a hygiene class and one in English usage. Supper was another fun time, mealtime being the only time we could talk to the boys. Some of the chaperons acted as though we were overstepping the bounds of proper decorum for young girls by doing so, but we didn't pay much attention to them.

By eight in the evening we girls were already changed into our nightgowns and had our teeth brushed. Then we sat in a semicircle on the floor around the desk at one end of the dorm. At this time every evening Dr. Del Mundo would make her rounds inquiring about our health. Then one of the mothers would read aloud to us from a book of poetry, or some other classic deemed suitable. Just before lights-out we answered roll call with "yes" or "no." I couldn't figure out what everyone was answering to when their name was called.

"Yes. Yes. Yes," Bridget groaned as though her patience had been tried once too often.

"Three times?" asked the chaperon, obviously concerned about Bridget.

"No," replied the group's rebel in a tight voice. "I just think it's being too nosy to ask us whether or not we've had a BM today."

So that was it! I was in complete agreement with Bridget. If they treated us like small children here, it wasn't going to be any fun at all. My next birthday would make me a teenager, and I wanted desperately to be treated like a grown-up.

A beastly hot summer finally gave way to the rainy season one day in June. We all ran excitedly out into the courtyard after class that day, to stand in the first shower of the season. It was known to be a better cure for heat rash than calamine lotion. It felt so good to have the cool water run down my face and into my mouth. Soon my hair was dripping, and my clothes soaking wet. The nuns and employees watching us from inside seemed to enjoy it as much as we did. To most of us, it was an old custom marking the end of the hot season.

Mother came to see us regularly and always brought us something extra to eat. Dad could only come once in a great while; the Japanese were not keeping their promise. Mother was growing bigger and heavier. Dad seemed a little thinner each time we saw him. Carole and I were simply growing.

The rainy season spawned a lot of illness in the dormitories. We had continuing bouts with colds and sore throats. Dr. Del Mundo still came every day to see us, but there was not much she could do without medicines. The doctor told Mother and Dad that my tonsils were nearing the point where a tonsillectomy would be necessary.

As bad as the situation was in regards to the medicine and medical care available at the time, my folks were afraid it might become worse. So they did what they could through our family doctor in STIC, through Dr. Del Mundo and family friends among the Filipinos. The result was that I was taken to St. Luke's Hospital to have my tonsils out in early October.

Mother had already taken up residence there at the urging of our family doctor, Dr. Fletcher. Her time to deliver was near, and he was afraid she would have trouble getting to the hospital at night, if need be, after curfew. It was wonderful to have Mother there with me. After surgery I awoke to her pretty face hovering over me. She coddled and babied me, while taking care of my every need. When there was nothing else to do for me, she read to me. I couldn't talk, so I really wasn't much company to her, but I filled her time of waiting. When I returned to Holy Ghost, Mother was still waiting. Several days after the big event, we learned we had a baby brother, Peter Sheldon, born on October 14. For many weeks Mother didn't visit us.

The day before my thirteenth birthday, in late November, news came that Carole and I were to be given a one-day pass to visit Mother. We were actually going home for the first time in almost a year! I could hardly sleep the night before, I was so excited. At eight the next morning Pascencia called for us at the convent. Sister Magdalene, the Mother Superior, gave us our pass and wished us a safe trip across town.

As soon as I stepped outside, Pascencia wished me a happy birthday. Carole and I both mobbed her with hugs. Laughing, she managed to push us off so she could see us better. "You big girls now," she said in surprise.

"Pas," I asked, looking around, "where is our carriage? You didn't walk, did you?"

"Yes," she said, still laughing about our exuberant greeting. "We walk home also."

"Let's get started then," chimed in Carole.

So off we went with our arms linked through Pas's, as if we were the Three Musketeers. We asked a million questions about everybody: family, servants, and neighbors. The epitome of her name, she answered every one patiently, only to be asked more. The morning was warm and muggy with angry-looking clouds boiling up in every direction. A typhoon had crossed the island south of Manila a few days earlier and left some wind damage and a thoroughly soaked city. Proof of that was still evident everywhere: mud washed across sidewalks, and huge puddles blocked our path.

It was almost like before the war, going somewhere with Pas. She used to accompany us everywhere as our chaperon. A Spanish custom, the use of chaperons lingered on in the Philippines even after the Americans came in 1900.

"Georgia, look down the street there," Carole said, pointing straight ahead of us. "What is that hanging on the light pole?"

Grabbing our hands, Pascencia said, "Come quick. We cross the street." She almost pulled us to the other side. We still couldn't see what it was, but we were curious about it because everyone else on the street did the same thing we did to avoid passing near it.

As we drew almost even with the large object swaying and twisting in the light breeze, I suddenly realized what I was seeing. "It's a man!" I gasped, unable to pull my eyes away. "A dead man. The Japanese killed him." I was certain of the indictment without having to ask.

"You girls don't look," scolded Pas. "You have bad dreams, by and by."

As if we had not heard her, we continued to stare in horrified fascination. Carole sounded nearly strangled when she said, "There are flies all over his face, Georgia. Why doesn't someone do something?"

Then the revolting odor of decaying flesh hit us full in the face. Gagging and coughing, Carole and I started to run away from the scene. Pas quickly caught up with us.

"Do not run," she commanded with rare severity. "If you run, Japanese might stop us to ask why." Now her voice pleaded with us to mind her. "Your mother said we should not do anything to attract the attention of soldiers."

"Okay, Pas," I agreed. "But let's walk as fast as we can for a while." As I covered my nose and mouth with a handkerchief, I mumbled, "Don't tell Mother what we saw."

The nearer we got to home, the harder it was to keep from running. We did see several soldiers along the way, but none of them seemed to take any notice of us. Once we reached our front steps, however, we raced each other up.

Mother and Lola were as happy to see us as we were to see them. After wishing me "many more," Lola commented on how much we had grown since she last saw us. Mother promised me a birthday tea party later.

"When can we see the baby?" wondered Carole as she glanced toward Mother's room.

"Let's tiptoe in to see if he's still asleep," whispered Mother, motioning us to follow.

We filed quietly into the bedroom and gazed over at the baby bed. Awake already and aware of our approach, two shiny black eyes turned in our direction.

"Oh, he sees us!" exclaimed Carole. "Can I hold him?" She was too excited to wait for an answer and reached for him herself.

Disappointed I hadn't asked first, I could only wait my turn. "What shall we call him, Pete or Peter or what?" I asked casually, while I stroked his plump cheek.

"I think we'll call him Pete," said Mother as she put him in my arms.

He was so soft and warm, and smelled of bath powder. When he took hold of my finger and gave me a little smile, I fell in love with him. Babies were great!

We had a wonderful time at home that day, what with being able to take care of Pete and the special lunch fixed for us. In the afternoon, we tried on some of the clothes that had been left behind in January, but found that most of them were too small. We spent a few minutes in the servants' quarters visiting with Aurora. Then it was time for my birthday party. Mother prepared a special treat for me: a lace tablecloth with linen napkins, our best china, and flowers in a vase. None of those things were part of our primitive life in camp or of the spartan one at Holy Ghost. For an hour I blotted those places out of my mind and relived a happier time.

By four in the afternoon Mother was gathering up the things we would be taking back with us. One last hug for everyone, and we were ready to leave with Jose.

Mother kissed us, then turning to our trusty servant, said, "Jose, please take good care of the girls."

"Yes, Mum," he replied. "We be very careful now."

Jose knew a shortcut and had us back at Holy Ghost in plenty of time for him to return before the curfew.

sneaked a bite in our dorm after each meal. Besides being tasty and nutritious, peanut butter makes a wonderful trade item. Two boys on the third floor somehow found out we had a jar of it. They promised us anything they had for some.

After lights-out at night Jim and Paul would lower a piece of string from their window directly above ours. At the end of it was a handkerchief tied to form a little pouch. Inside was a piece of bread, which the boys had saved from their supper earlier. The agreement was to tear the piece of bread in half, put a bit of the precious spread on their half, and send it back up in the sling. We could then fix our piece and divide it between us.

Sometimes a "love note" accompanied the bread and gave us the right to claim we had boyfriends. The rest of the older girls didn't remain envious for very long. They soon worked out similar trade deals with other boys. It wasn't long until we girls were reading each other's notes and giggling like a bunch of silly fools, all of which finally came to the attention of Mrs. Duvall. She scolded us severely and tried to shame us by calling us "hussies." We didn't understand the word, but her tone cut us deeply.

Dad was released from jail in mid-February and came to see us again. He brought some good news and some bad news. The good news was that the International Red Cross had, in early January, distributed relief packages to all internees: canned foods, dried milk, sugar, and many other items were included. Dad was keeping our boxes in camp for us.

Dad's bad news was a rumor that the Japanese were preparing to open a new internment camp and would be sending there some, if not all, of the present population from STIC. The rumor did not include where the new camp was or when the transfer would take place. Rumors being rumors, internees knew they couldn't believe them completely, and yet they frequently were found to contain more than just a bit of truth. The possibility that there was some truth in this rumor was clearly making Dad nervous because his family was scattered across the city. Who could tell when the Japanese might ship him off to another camp, leaving a wife and three children behind?

"I think, before long, I probably should bring you girls, Pete, and your mother back into camp," Dad said as he fanned himself with his hat. "If people are going to be shifted around, we ought to be together. That way we would stand a better chance of being sent to the same place."

"Dad," I interrupted his musing, "Dr. Del Mundo is leaving her post here. Retiring, I guess."

"Will there be another doctor assigned here in her place?" Dad wondered.

"She didn't tell us that," I answered. "Did you hear that three of the mothers and twenty of the children here were taken back to camp about a month ago?"

"No. Must have been while I was locked up." Dad looked concerned. "That settles it. I will start procedures tomorrow to have Mother and Pete brought into camp. I'll get them settled in before I request you girls be returned."

"How soon will we see you again?" asked Carole.

"I'll try to come in two weeks," Dad said. "But I don't want your mother coming here anymore. The Japanese picked up about fifty people the other day for no apparent reason. They had legitimate passes, just as she does, but they were held overnight in a police station anyway. I don't trust them. You don't know when they may change their minds."

While our days at Holy Ghost now seemed numbered, life continued in the same way: dull routine much of the time. It would be better back in STIC. We could be with Mother and the rest of the family again, and help take care of Pete, whom we hadn't seen in over two months. He must have grown a lot since then. We waited impatiently for our call.

One day Bridget and I were sitting in the garden talking during the little free time we had before supper.

"Have you noticed the fruit trees over there in the nuns' garden?" I asked. It was a small walled-in area where the sisters went to walk and meditate.

"Yeah," she answered with a wicked grin. "I'd like to have some of those limes or an orange, wouldn't you?"

"The sisters wouldn't know it if only a few pieces were missing, would they?" I wondered idly. "Citrus fruit is good for us, isn't it?"

Bridget agreed. "We really ought to have more citrus fruit to eat." Her green eyes were snapping with deviltry. "How about it?" she prodded me. "Let's try a sneak attack on the sisters' garden tonight."

Suddenly wishing I had not mentioned the fruit, I asked, "All by ourselves? At night?"

Disgusted, Bridget said, "Count me out for a daytime raid."

"Maybe Peggy and Janet would want to be in with us," I said hopefully, a firm believer in the old adage "safety in numbers."

"No," said Bridget, completely in charge now. "Either it's just the two of us or I'm not going."

"Okay," I demurred. "Just me and you." Already I was becoming a little jittery.

"Don't tell anyone," she cautioned me. "Not even Carole. After lights-out tonight, I'll wait an hour or so, until I think everyone is asleep. Then I'll come get you." Jumping up at the sound of the dinner bell, she giggled excitedly, "This is going to be great fun!"

It was beginning to sound like quite an adventure. My friend's enthusiasm was infectious. Later, after everyone was in bed, I found myself waiting impatiently while the big clock downstairs chimed every fifteen minutes. There wasn't any other sound; surely everyone was asleep by now. Why didn't Bridget come? I dozed off for a few minutes. Then a hand was suddenly clamped over my mouth, and Bridget whispered in my ear, "Don't make any noise. Let's go!"

Barefoot, we crept out of the dorm and down the hall to the staircase. It was so dark I felt sure we would fall down the stairs. I reached out for Bridget as I asked frantically in a stage whisper, "Where are you?"

"Shhhh!" she hissed ahead of me. "Hurry up!"

On the ground floor we felt our way along the wall to the door leading out to the courtyard. Creeeak! Those rusty old hinges would wake everyone in the building.

"Oh gosh," fumed Bridget. "I didn't think about the moon shining so bright tonight."

"Somebody will see us," I fretted. "It's as bright as day out here."

"Shhhh! They won't see us if you don't wake them up," she scolded. "Let's hurry."

She pulled her nightgown way up so she could run. I followed suit, and we darted for the nearest tree. While I paused to catch my breath, I gazed at the moon. It looked so big and so near, as if a huge balloon were sitting on the garden wall. Its radiance bathed everything in a soft, pearly white glow. When Bridget ran from tree to tree, she reminded me of a ghostly butterfly flitting here and there in search of flowers.

"Psstt," she whistled softly. "Come on!"

I caught up with her at the iron gate leading into the sisters' garden. Afraid it too would be squeaky, we climbed gingerly over it. Then we hurried to the nearest tree.

"You climb this one," Bridget told me. "And shake it hard when you get up there."

Not knowing what else to do with my voluminous nightgown, I pulled it up to just below my fanny and tied a big knot in it. Climbing trees was what I used to do best and enjoy the most when I was younger. This would be easy!

Up past the lower two branches, I shook the tree as hard as I could. The leaves made so much noise, it sounded like a typhoon-force wind blowing. We were making far too much noise. We would be found out any minute!

Bridget was waving her arms for me to stop. "Quit," she called softly. "It's not working. Let's go try one more."

By the time I reached the next tree she was already up and shaking it for all she was worth. Down came a few native limes. I quickly gathered them up and stuffed them in the knot of my nightgown.

"That's enough," I whispered up at her. My heart was pounding with a belated realization: we were not only stealing, we were in a forbidden garden. "Let's get the heck out of here!

Georgia, behind, and her sister, Carole, in the jungle around the gold mine at Tagkawayan.

Dad and Mother, taken before the war in Lola and Grandpa Jake's garden in Manila.

Dad and Mother, Sheldon & Dorothy Barnes, on their 50th anniversary in 1978.

Living room, or *sala*, of Lola and Grandpa Jake's home in Manila. The Barnes family met here with Lola just before the fall of Manila in January 1942.

Santo Tomas University - Main Building

Drawn by fellow internee M. Oftedahl. Taken from
Santo Tomas Internment Camp
by Frederic H. Stevens, Stratford House, 1946.

A prewar snapshot of Georgia in her Filipina native dress, the *balintawok*.

Georgia on the left and Carole behind Mother. Taken before the war, on the front steps of Auntie and Uncle Dick's house at the mine near Tagkawayan.

Bridget dropped to the ground. "A light just came on in the sisters' quarters," she breathed, frightened. "We'd better hurry."

We scurried back to the gate and through it, not taking the time to climb over. Once inside the building, we didn't waste any time returning to our room.

At the foot of my bed I whispered, "Did you shut the garden gate?"

"No!" she squeaked in alarm. "I forgot! Did you close the door downstairs?"

"I don't think so," I answered. "I was only thinking of getting back to bed before someone caught us."

"It's too late to go back," Bridget growled. "We're in for it now." Her parting words were, "You hide the fruit."

The next day Bridget and I were especially diligent at our school work. All day we wondered when retribution would strike. We were certain our faces, if studied carefully, would testify to our guilt. Late in the afternoon, we retrieved the few limes I had hidden among my socks and took them to the bathroom. Together in a stall we sampled them.

Bridget made the most awful face I ever saw and grabbed her throat. It was a minute before she could speak. "They're too sour!"

I took a little taste of one and dropped it in the toilet. "We can't eat these," I told her. "It must take a ton of sugar to turn them into limeade."

The most depressing part of all was that we were probably going to get into trouble for something that tasted terrible. Five little unripe limes were flushed away. We relaxed a little with the evidence gone. At least they couldn't prove it was us now.

That night after roll call Mrs. Duvall announced that the nuns had reason to believe someone had left the building and entered their garden the night before. Her eyes slowly went around the room.

"Both of those activities are strictly against the rules," she intoned as her eyes lingered for an extra moment on Bridget's face. Then she told us that if that sort of thing happened again, it could very well be the cause of all the children being sent back to STIC. Luckily we were not discovered, but to say we had learned a good lesson was a patent understatement.

In early March Sister Magdalene told Carole and me that we would be going back to Santo Tomas with the next busload of returning parents. She wished us good luck and said she was glad we had been able to stay at Holy Ghost even if it was for only a short while.

To show how sorry they were that we were leaving, our friends planned a little going-away party on our last night at Holy Ghost. After roll call, the girls produced whatever extra food their families had been able to bring them. We shared with each other; no one was left out, not even those who had nothing to contribute. We had fun that night singing songs and playing guessing games. It was a real party.

Dad didn't come with the parents from STIC the next day. He and the rest of the family would be waiting for us in front of the main building when our bus pulled to a stop. Holy Ghost had been a pleasant experience; it had given us a safe refuge for many months that included adequate food, education, and companionship among friends.

While living there I had become a young lady in the physical sense of the word; no longer growing taller, I was instead filling out in all the right places. Being away from my parents for an extended period of time had contributed to my maturing. But now I was anxious to be with them once again. When the bus stopped at the main building, I was the first to alight. Everyone was there to greet us: Dad, Mom and Pete, Auntie and Uncle Dick. We hadn't seen Auntie and Uncle Dick for such a long time. They looked so good to me in spite of their thinness.

"Can I hold Pete now?" I begged. "It's been ages!"

Mother put him in my arms. "Gosh! How heavy he is now."

"Do we get to see what you have done to the shanty since we left?" Carole asked. "Or do we see our new room first?"

"Let's take your things to the room first," Dad said, picking up the suitcases. "Then we'll go to the shanty."

So we trooped through the main building, in the front door and out the back, which was the shortest route to the annex. Once there, Mother led the way around a small patio to our room, on the east side of the long, one-story building. Uncle Dick had made each of us a wooden bed, which was topped with the necessary mosquito net. Mother's bed was just like ours. Pete's bed was a typical one for the tropics, enclosed on all four sides with screen. There was a screened lid that could be pulled up to close the bed against insects and yet allow air to circulate.

I was relieved to see there were two other girls about my age in the room. I wouldn't be the only teenager in a room full of mothers and little children.

"How do you do?" said one friendly girl with a heavy Scottish accent. "My name is Bella Mary Edith Muir."

"I'm Georgia," I told her, amused with the impressive length of her name. "I hope we can be friends."

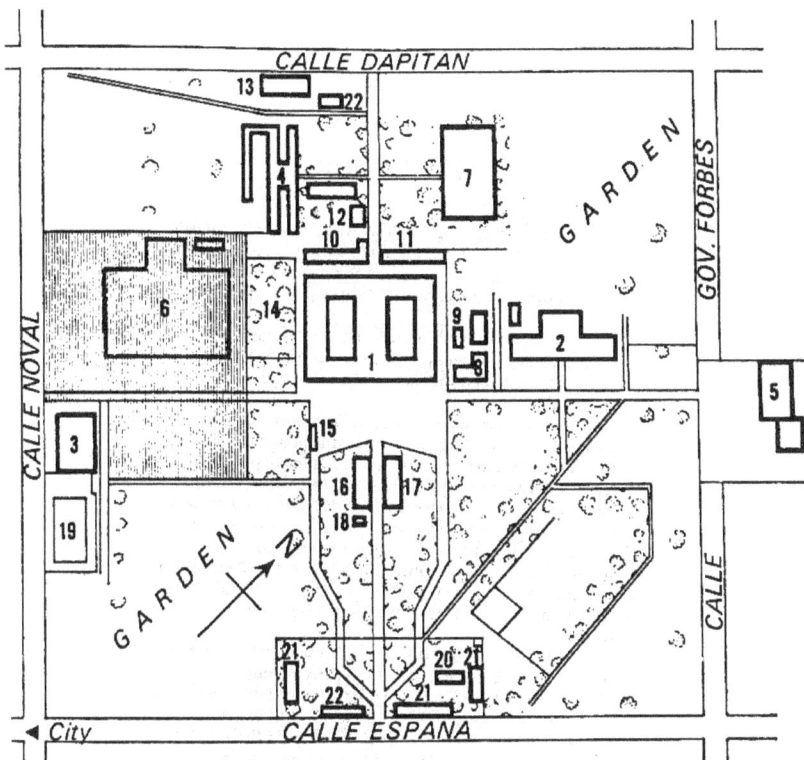

	Santo Tomas Internment Camp
	L E G E N D

1	Main Building	12	Finance and Supply Bodegas
2	Education Building	13	Japanese Food Bodega
3	Gymnasium Building	14	Padre's Garden
4	Annex	15	Dave Harvey's Stage
5	Santa Catalina Hospital	16	Classrooms
6	Dominican Seminary and Church	17	Plumbing Shop and Sanitation Bodega
7	Isolation Hospital	18	Shoe and Cot Repairing
8	Commandant's Office	19	Reserve Water Supply (swimming pool)
9	Soft Diet Kitchen	20	Package Shed
10	Camp Outside Kitchen	21	Japanese Guard Quarters
11	Dining Sheds	22	Japanese Guard House (office)

(Shaded portions represent the restricted area, about 11 acres)

Taken from *The Santo Tomas Story* by A.V.H Hartendorp
(McGraw-Hill, 1964)

Chapter 9

We left our things in the room and took a leisurely stroll toward the east side of the main building, where our shanty stood. I noticed that the general appearance of those internees we met along the way was quite different from what it had been several months before. At that time few of them would have gone about in public wearing the garb everyone was now sporting.

Under present conditions, however, their attire could only be considered sensible. Conical-shaped native hats with their wide brims would serve as umbrellas in rainy or sunny weather. Native wooden shoes were cool and kept one's feet off the ground. Men wore shorts and no shirts. Women, at first forbidden by the Japanese to wear shorts, were now enjoying them, and halters as well. Small children ran around in the barest of essentials. The internment camp was clearly occupied by a people intent on making life as tolerable as possible for however long it might be necessary.

It was also plain that the camp itself had changed. It had a look of permanence about it. Almost all of the areas previously open were now filled with shanties. The only open space of any size in the camp was the main plaza and the shaded lawn extending from there down to the main gate. Internee construction crews had roofed the dining sheds behind the main building for the rainy season. Where once our shanty stood along with just a few others, there was a sea of thatched roofs so close together, one might jump from one to another without ever touching the ground.

In single file we followed Dad into a warren of narrow footpaths. The paths had names, and the different areas or groups of shanties had names and an elected mayor. Our shanty was on Bum's Alley in Froggy Bottom. Each shanty was different from every other in size and shape as well as in the variety of materials used in its construction. I didn't recognize our shanty until we stepped inside and I raised my eyes to the ceiling; there were the movie posters I remembered. Dad and Uncle Dick had extended the thatched roof, thereby giving it a wider, lower overhang. We had to stoop under it to enter. They had also built a moveable wall that could be used against blowing rain. The men in our family seemed to appreciate our enthusiastic approval of their efforts. They both beamed.

"Now I want you girls to meet our new neighbors," Mother said. "I don't think they were here when you left."

The shanty immediately to the north of ours was a very nice one, built off the ground in the native style. "Anybody home?" she called just as the door opened.

"Girls, I want you to meet Ronnie and Maria Laing. These are the people who make the peanut butter and coco honey Dad sent to you at Holy Ghost."

"It was really good," I complimented them. "I'm Georgia and this is my sister, Carole. Could we watch you make it sometime?"

"Certainly. We'd be glad to show you," Ronnie said in a British accent.

"Come any time at all." Maria sounded Spanish.

Mother took us next across Bum's Alley, which was wide enough right there to have four shanties open onto it. Facing our shanty was a small lean-to affair, where three smiling people were seated at their table watching us.

"Which one is Georgia and which one is Carole?" asked the round-faced woman, in an accent I couldn't quite identify. She had trouble making the soft *g* sound.

Mother introduced us and then told us, "This is Jan and Jo DeBree. They are Dutch and were caught in Manila on a visit from the Dutch East Indies."

"We are glad to meet you," said Jo heartily. "Jan, he don't speak the English much." She indicated her husband. "I don't so much either, but I'm not afraid to try." She laughed and nudged him in the ribs. He smiled, but continued to puff on his pipe. He obviously could not be made to speak before he was ready.

Mother teased him, "He knows English better than I know Dutch. He'll surprise us someday."

Then she turned to the other lady at the table and said, "This is Pat McDonald from England. She and Jo room together in the main building. Pat's working on Jan's English. With her for a teacher, he's bound to learn sooner or later." Pat stood up to shake our hands. My, but she was tall and extremely thin. Her face, too angular and bony to be pretty, took on real warmth when she smiled. "It's a pleasure to meet you both. Your mother has told us so much about you, we feel we know you already."

We soon settled back into the old routine at STIC. Our days were full and busy. After the work was done there really wasn't much time left over in which to get bored. Our laundry was no longer being sent out to Lola. Our old laundress, Aurora, had returned to her family in the provinces, and Lola had been unable to hire another one. So we took our dirty clothes to the outdoor laundry shed on the west side of the main building to do the family wash.

Once a week every room had to be emptied of everything, beds and all, and the room scrubbed with disinfectant. Not all rooms were cleaned on the same day, or there would have been no place in the halls to put everything. If it wasn't raining on cleaning day, we had to sun our bedding and go over every piece, inspecting seams and folds for bedbugs. Contests for the cleanest rooms were hard fought, with the winner in each building broadcast over the public address system. Even the tables and benches in the dining shed had to be scrubbed and disinfected on a regular basis because bedbugs also lived in the joints and cracks of wood.

School was out for the summer; March, April, and May were the hottest months of the year. Sometimes twice a day Mother would send me with Pete to spend an hour or two on the shady lawn across from the main building. It was as cool a place as could be found anywhere in camp. A blanket spread on the grass made a soft place for Pete to play or nap, while I read and fanned away the insects.

"What a darling baby," said a girl, casting a shadow across my book. "How old is it?"

I looked up to see a girl with a friendly, freckled face smiling at me. "Pete's almost six months old," I replied, warming to her. "Would you like to hold him?"

In this simple way began a friendship that was unforgettable if brief. Her name was Grace Branbles, though she said I should call her Bunny as her family did. Bunny was from Australia, but had lived in Manila for several years. She was a year or so older than I, with sandy hair and a round face. She, too, had attended Bordner School before the war, but because she was two years ahead of me, we had not met.

Bunny and I became fixtures under that tree. We talked hour after hour about all the things young girls talk about. Our thoughts were so much in tune that we could finish each other's sentences or start to say the same thing at the same time. Those many hours we spent getting to know each other and sharing our innermost thoughts remain in my memory as an idyllic period amidst the chaos of war.

When the internee entertainment committee was allowed to put on barn dances for the young people, Bunny and I went together. She taught me how to waltz and two-step. We had a lot of fun, but increasingly Japanese soldiers would appear at the fringes of the audience and make everyone uneasy.

One time when the dance was almost over, Bunny whispered in my ear, "Oh, ohhh! Look over there."

A soldier was striding into the throng of dancers. There was a collective catching of breath from the sidelines. As the dancers noticed him among them, they fell away, leaving a wide path in his wake. He didn't seem to notice anything but the girl who had caught his attention. When he took hold of her arm, she turned startled eyes on him and covered her mouth to keep from screaming.

A woman, who must have been the girl's mother, ran to her defense. The poor girl was being pulled this way and that, while her mother protested in English and the soldier shouted in Japanese. The scene had all the volatility of a volcano about to erupt. Then an officer entered the picture and promptly put a stop to the terrifying episode. Predictably, the entertainment committee and parents agreed there would be no more dances.

Early in May 1943 the rumors, heard months before about moving some or all of the internees to a new camp, were heard again. People were dismayed at the thought of the hardship and upheaval such a move would cause. They were doubtful that any other place could be adapted to the overall comfort of so many people as had Santo Tomas University. When it was officially announced that eight hundred men would be sent to Los Banos in a week, the camp was in turmoil. Uncle Dick's name was on the list. So were Bunny's two brothers. Auntie was distraught. We were all upset that our family would soon be separated again.

The official notice said that families would be separated only until the men could build barracks to house two or three thousand people; then the wives could join their men in Los Banos. But the fear that this was a Japanese trick to eventually leave all the women and children alone haunted everyone. The work was supposed to take only two or three months, but that did not take into account that the rainy season was about to start again. No one felt sure that those men who were leaving would ever be seen or heard from again.

Three days before their departure the Japanese closed the package line indefinitely. The camp was totally isolated. In retrospect it was easy to understand why: the Japanese did not want anyone on the outside to know there would soon be a transfer of internees, for fear someone might try to aid an escape.

It was while the package line was closed that we began to rely on the Red Cross relief packages received the previous Christmas. Fortunately, Dad and Uncle Dick had stored them virtually intact, though some people had nothing left. After the first six months of internment, the Japanese had been providing rations for the camp, but they were so meager that supplemental food was almost a necessity. So we used some of that food sparingly.

On the morning the men were to leave, the whole camp was awakened at four for breakfast at daybreak. Afterward families gathered together on the main plaza. It was a quiet, sober crowd.

"Sheldon, I leave Evelyn in your care," Uncle Dick said solemnly. "We'll work hard to build those barracks as fast as we can." Looking down at Auntie close by his side, he squeezed her shoulder and added, "I'll sure do my part."

"I'll join you just as soon as they let me," Auntie told him with a forced smile. "Whether the barracks are ready or not."

"Here they come," someone in the crowd said. Everyone turned to watch the line of trucks roll through the front gate. As they neared the plaza, a hush fell over the throng. The only sound was that of the trucks, as, brakes squealing and gears grinding, they stopped.

"Girls, give me a quick hug and kiss," Uncle Dick said as he reached for both of us at the same time. "You'll keep your aunt from being lonesome, won't you?" His face was twisted; sometimes when you want more than anything to smile, it ends up looking wrong side out.

"I'll learn how to play cribbage," I volunteered, blinking back the tears. "But I know I'll never be as good as you are at it."

"Good-bye, Dorothy," Uncle Dick told Mother, patting her on the back. "Take good care of Pete. He's the only nephew I have."

Turning to Dad, he shook his hand and spoke through tight lips. "Until we meet again."

They continued to shake hands, unwilling to make the break. "Best of luck, Porter," Dad finally said.

Quietly, all over the plaza, men were climbing into the trucks to stand staring at their loved ones, as if committing their faces to memory. Uncle Dick took Auntie in his arms. Completely enveloping her, he buried his face in her hair. They clung to each other as though it would be the last time ever. Then, tearing himself away, he quickly boarded the nearest truck.

Over the din of the truck motors, faintly at first, but then growing louder until the music was unmistakable, we could hear "Onward, Christian Soldiers" coming over the public address system. That hymn and then a march were played while the convoy drove around the plaza and down the street lined with people. Farewells filled the air as the last truck disappeared through the gate.

Two days later the package line opened again. The basket that day held a dozen duck eggs and a sizable amount of coarse salt. The note from Lola told us she would be sending a large container in which Dad could put the eggs for pickling. Sure enough, the next day Jose brought an oversize clay pot with more fresh eggs. With the salt and fresh water Dad made a brine solution strong enough to float an egg. Then he placed all the eggs in the brine and weighted them down with a plate and a stone set on top. Covered with the lid to slow evaporation, the eggs would stay fresh enough to eat for an indefinite period of time.

From that time on the duck eggs we did not use the day Lola sent them went into the brine for future use. We had no access to refrigeration. Duck eggs, from that locale at least, had a very distinct fishy flavor, but were nonetheless an important source of protein in our diet. Our hunger later would render the fishy flavor of no importance at all.

In spite of the eight hundred men taken to Los Banos, the population in STIC was still growing and went over 3,600 around the first of June 1943. The overcrowding was partly a result of the reinternment of many of the people who had been released temporarily for health reasons. Many of them now probably returned voluntarily because food on the outside was becoming scarcer. Also, Allied nationalities from distant provinces and islands were still being rounded up and brought to Santo Tomas for internment.

As a result of the overcrowding the Japanese commandant gave permission for four hundred men and boys to sleep in their shanties. Dad was not one of them, simply because our shanty was not large enough for a bed. Neither did it afford any privacy for changing clothes; it was open on all sides. The time for enlarging an existing shanty was already past, as ours was hemmed in by others on three sides. So Dad continued to quarter in the Education Building, Auntie in the main building, and the rest of us in the annex.

Early in June a typhoon brought an extremely wet week. Other than making life somewhat more difficult and dismal, it caused no real damage. With the onset of the rainy season school opened inside rather than outdoors, as it had when we attended more than a year before.

The lower grades, so the small children wouldn't have to climb stairs, held classes in a shed that had been recently built across the plaza from the main building. Seventh through twelfth grades were moved to the enclosed rooms on the roof of the main building, which were four floors and eight long flights of stairs up. It was quite a climb to make each morning on a breakfast of one ladle of cracked cornmeal mush with no milk and a spoon of sugar only every other day.

The shortage of food and noticeable drop in its quality in the first eighteen months had caused a wholesale loss of weight and a definite downturn in the physical well-being of nearly every internee. Those suffering the most were the elderly and people already chronically ill before internment. What milk was still available in cans was doled out very stringently to babies and toddlers. Our family was remarkably healthy in the beginning, and so had not suffered noticeably during this early period.

If food was difficult to obtain, clothing, while not as important, was simply impossible to get. All of our clothing from home had been sent to us the previous year. What we had not worn out, Carole and I had outgrown. Clothes were patched, at first in an effort to hide the tears and worn places. Later it just didn't matter; we patched them with whatever came to hand.

Some enterprising internee obtained, through the package line, a quantity of grocery store twine wound on large cones. That commodity was traded and exchanged endlessly. Mrs. Muir, our roommate in the annex, was the first person I saw with some.

"What are you making?" I asked her one day. She was knitting with the string, and making a dainty, lacy item.

"Unmentionables, me dearie," replied that good Scotswoman with a mischievous smile. "Bloomers! Panties! Whatever you want to call them."

"Really?" I was impressed with a pair of the finished article she held up to show me.

"Not only that, me lovely," she whispered behind her hand. "Look at this, will you?" Whereupon she produced a bra from her suitcase. It was a work of art, crocheted in concentric circles from the same string.

"Gosh, I wish I could do that," I said enviously. "I could sure use the panties, and I could sort of use one of those, too," I pointed to the bra.

"Can you knit or crochet?" she asked.

"I don't crochet, but I can knit, though not as well as you. Would you teach me how to knit your way?" I begged eagerly. "It looks like it goes so much faster."

"If you'll get the string and the needles," she assured me, "I'll gladly show you how I knit. I could make you a bra for enough string to make Bella one, too."

I asked Dad if he could trade something out of my Red Cross kit for a cone of the coveted string. When I explained why, he agreed to see what he could do. In two days, at a cost I don't remember, he presented it to me.

Day after day I struggled, under Mrs. Muir's tutelage, with the new method. Finally it became second nature, and the pair of panties I was working on was finished. They had a pretty design with many little holes for coolness. As previously agreed to, Mrs. Muir made two bras, one for me and one for Bella. The best that could be said for the entire project was that I learned a more efficient way to knit, which would serve me well in later life.

As for the handmade finery, of which I was very proud, it filled a need, but I think I would not have been more uncomfortable had I worn a burlap sack next to my skin. With each laundering, fortunately, the string garments became softer, and I became accustomed to the roughness.

Chapter 10

After Uncle Dick went to Los Banos I spent a lot of time with Auntie, when Dad or Mother didn't need me. Sometimes after supper we would sit on her bed and play cards. Once I learned how to play cribbage, we could talk and joke as we played. But occasionally we played Russian Bank, which is solitaire played by two people together. During those quiet games, while making plays almost automatically, my mind would wander back to some particularly happy time before the war.

I could conjure up the blindingly white, sandy beach of Matabungkay, where our family went to swim and picnic. It was far from the city, and we usually had the beach to ourselves, except for a few local Filipinos. We swam in the bluest of waters, basked in the shimmering rays of the tropical sun, and sometimes were sunburned bad enough to hurt for several days. Matabungkay was a tropical paradise, and we reveled in the enjoyment of it.

"Georgia, dear," Auntie said, breaking my reverie. "You could put the eight on that nine." Then in a moment she chided herself, "I shouldn't be telling you what to do; I forgot to move this jack over to that queen."

"I guess I don't really have my mind on it tonight," I apologized.

"I don't either," she admitted. "Why don't we just talk until roll call? Do you want to tell me what you were thinking?"

"Oh, just about when we used to take a picnic and spend the day down at the beach," I answered reluctantly, afraid that sharing such a vivid memory might diminish it. "What were you thinking about?" I asked her. "Uncle Dick?"

"Yes, of course. As I often do." Auntie gazed over my shoulder, and with a dreamy little smile playing around her lips, she began reminiscing. "I was thinking about when I first met your Uncle. Did you know our first date was a blind date?"

"No, I sure didn't," I answered, immediately interested. "Where did you go?"

"He took me to dinner at the Army and Navy Club." Auntie was quite animated. "He presented me with a gardenia corsage and pinned it on my dress."

Imagining myself being treated in such a romantic fashion, I was hungry for details. "Then what did you do?"

"Well, after dinner we danced until very late." Musing silently to herself for a moment, she added, "And then he bought a lei to put around my neck. It had such a sweet scent; I can almost smell the flowers now. It was the loveliest time I ever had."

"I can remember your wedding in the Union Church. Dr. Foley made it such a beautiful ceremony," I recalled. "It was the only wedding I have ever been to. You looked so pretty and Uncle Dick was so handsome. When I get married I want a wedding just like yours."

"I hope your wedding will be everything you ever dream it will be, my dear. And more." Auntie smiled indulgently. "But that is several years away yet; you'll have lots of time after the war to finish your schooling, meet the right man, and then plan your wedding and future."

"Do you really think the war will ever be over?" I asked seriously, searching her face for any sign of hope.

Auntie clasped my hands in hers and looked straight into my eyes. "Honey, I know it will; I believe that with all my strength. Look at the people around you. Everyone goes about his daily routine with the certain knowledge that this is just temporary. If folks didn't believe that, they wouldn't have the heart to get out of bed every morning."

"But we've been prisoners for a year and a half now," I interjected, not quite able to see the same future she did. "How much longer is it going to last?"

"Now, that is a much harder question," Auntie laughed. "I could tell you anything you wanted to hear, but it would just be a guess." Squeezing my hands harder, she grew serious once again. "Look at it this way, dear: every sunset brings us one day closer to liberation, and with every sunrise our hope is born anew."

Auntie's words of trust in the future filled me as surely as rainwater fills a reservoir. Her intense resilience was surprising and infectious.

Impressed, I said, "I'll try to remember that." Then suddenly I remembered roll call. "What time is it?"

"You have exactly five minutes to get to your room," Auntie said. "Run, dear. I'll see you tomorrow."

That little talk with Auntie helped me a great deal. I resolved to stop having such a gloomy outlook. If Auntie really thought there was hope, then I would adopt the same attitude. One way to shorten the time between sunrise and sunset was to be busy. I would try to fill my time with enough activity to speed the day of liberation.

Not yet the age when work was required of me, I went looking for little jobs that would not only help pass the day, but might also benefit me in other ways as well.

Auntie told me of several ladies on her floor who, for one reason or another, wanted someone to take their toilet duty. When I inquired about the job, I got all the work I could handle in my spare time. It wasn't difficult work: handing out the maximum of two sheets of toilet paper to each bathroom visitor. Then, after each use of the toilet, I had to wipe the seat with a cloth wrung out of disinfectant. That part wasn't much fun, but the job was profitable. The women who could afford to hire out their share of camp work were generous to me. Sometimes I would earn a can of corned beef for an hour's duty every day for a week. Sometimes I was paid with a piece of secondhand clothing or a few small coins. Even though Dad didn't like my doing toilet duty for other people, he willingly used my earnings for the good of the whole family.

One day he said to me, "I asked the man in charge of the main kitchen if you could be on their serving crew."

"Gosh, what did he say?" I asked eagerly.

"He said he'd give you a try," Dad answered with the little smile that usually accompanied one of his wry jokes. "I had to tell him that you might be a bit too short on one end to reach over the counter."

"Oh, Dad!" I grinned. "I'll find something to stand on. That'll be a better job than washing toilets."

"Well, he said to be there fifteen minutes before the chow line opens in the morning." Dad patted me on the back. "I've already got a box for you. When you get there, step into the kitchen and call me. I'll bring it out for you."

Thus began several months of serving on the main chow line, twice a day. Dad produced an orange crate from somewhere, which made me appear almost as tall as the other servers. Except for the rice, which I never was allowed to serve, all the food was watery and had to be well stirred between each serving so that the solid pieces didn't settle out.

The man with the ticket punch would call out the number of tickets each person held as he came up to the counter. I was to give that person as many ladles full of food as he had tickets for. It wasn't long before the regulars in my line were giving me a hard time.

"Hey, shorty," a toothless old man, whom everyone called Buster, said that first night. "How about an extra dipper of that stuff?"

"I've already given you three," I said nervously. "Do you have four tickets?"

"Naw." He grinned widely. "Just wanted to see if you were a soft touch."

"Don't pay any attention to him," said the next man, with a note of sympathy. "He'd wheedle the last morsel of food away from his own grandmother if he could."

I acquired the habit of looking for Buster, and a few others who could be difficult to deal with. Some wanted to see me stir the pot while they watched. Others tried to coax me to not stir it at all and go straight to the bottom with the ladle for whatever might have settled there.

One elderly lady, who was already as thin as a toothpick, looked sadly at her portion for a moment and then said to me, "I didn't get a piece of meat with mine."

"That's because it's meatless stew tonight," I said as kindly as I could. "You should make a point to check the menu board; then you won't be disappointed."

Serving the imitation coffee in the morning was hard to do without scalding the hand holding the cup. I liked best to be one of the cereal servers. The cracked wheat or cornmeal mush were both thin enough to serve easily. At the same time, there was always some that clung to the sides of the kettle. If I clumsily brushed the back of my hand against the inside, some cereal would stick to me. When no one was looking, I quickly licked it off. I soon learned to be clumsy. Little licks could add up.

Finding something, anything, to eat was becoming a tough problem for everyone. No one ever had all they wanted. Malnutrition plagued all of us. Some especially unfortunate people already showed obvious symptoms of diseases directly related to poor and insufficient food. Dad's feet were swollen with beriberi. Later it would affect our whole family, with the swelling creeping up our legs. Some people also had the discolored skin patches of pellagra.

Hunger stalked the internees, while they in turn stalked the cats and dogs unfortunate enough to wander into our camp. About this time, the large flower beds, which had dotted the university campus, were dug up for the canna bulbs. They were found to be edible when sliced, soaked, and boiled. Or they could be dried in the sun and ground for flour. Even the banana palms were cut down and the core used to provide something to chew on. Weeds pulled in the camp gardens were awarded to the puller as extra food, although care had to be taken to not eat the poisonous ones.

Under these circumstances, we never questioned Dad about what he served in our shanty for lunch. Besides being a camp cook, he was our cook, working endlessly to turn the inedible into something palatable. Only rarely did Dad use anything from our Red Cross kits. It was his iron will, in the face of our continual hunger, that kept the life-saving rations in reserve against worse days to come.

In September rumors told of the Americans driving the Japanese out of first the Solomon Islands, then New Guinea. Rumors of this nature really buoyed the spirits of the internees. People thought it could not be much longer before the Americans retook the Philippines.

"With the Americans so close now, we could start using more of our canned foods, couldn't we, Dad?" I asked one day over a meager lunch of boiled weeds and tiny dried fish.

"You probably never knew about it because you were in Holy Ghost at the time," began Mother. "But about a year ago there were rumors that the marines had landed at Guadalcanal. And we're still here."

"Then I guess you could say the rumors are just so much wishful thinking," I grumbled as I carefully cut each of my three fish in half. They were so small, and the ration for each person so few, that we could not afford to throw away their heads. The trick to eating them, head, innards and all, was to pop a piece in your mouth, chew twice and swallow quickly. Of course it helped a lot to be otherwise occupied, as we were now, in interesting conversation.

Dad cleared his throat and told us quietly, "The rumors I tell you are not just rumors. They are actually news."

"Really, Dad?" Carole chortled, the look of disgust for the fish quickly fading from her face. "How do you know?"

"It is more or less common knowledge among internees that there is at least one radio receiver in camp. I'm not violating a confidence by telling you girls this, because I don't know who has it or where it is hidden. I just know that rumors from certain people can be relied upon."

"Just think of that!" I marveled. "Someone in camp is brave enough to hide a radio from the Japanese. That's why they're always searching through our rooms, isn't it?"

"No doubt," agreed Dad, adding very earnestly, "It could be extremely serious if a radio was found. That's why I won't tell you whose rumors I believe. I just wanted you to know that the camp has a source of news and the news is improving. I expect you girls to never say anything about what I have just told you."

"Gosh, Dad, we wouldn't tell a secret that important!" I promised. "But it is thrilling to know that the Americans are on their way back."

In November 1943 a typhoon struck Manila and dumped twenty-seven inches of rain on STIC in three days. A wind of sixty miles an hour drove the rain around and through the shuttered window of the annex. Our bedding was soaked. The electricity was off for over three days. Gas service for the kitchen was interrupted for a couple of days. Because city water became contaminated, it was shut off.

Life in camp, already difficult at best, became miserable. So many shanties were blown down that hundreds more people than usual were jammed into the buildings. There was no water for showers, and the toilets could be flushed only by carrying in buckets of water from the outside, where floodwater stood six feet deep in some places. Adding to the problem, kerosene and coconut-oil lanterns to light the halls and bathrooms at night made the air smoky and oppressive.

Because the kitchen could not function without gas, Dad was up all one night with the rest of the crew to build outdoor fireplaces on which to cook. They were made of stone and set under one of the dining sheds. By breakfast the next morning, we had our usual hot mush and black coffee. Being damp and chilled to the bone made us very thankful for that basic creature comfort.

When the sun finally came out a few days later, Dad and Auntie helped us spread all our things outside in the sunshine. Our shanty lost some of its roofing but had not suffered much real damage. We couldn't use it, however, for over a week; not until the water went down and the ground had a chance to dry.

There was one positive result of the typhoon: a new source of food was discovered. When rice was cooked in the outdoor fireplaces over charcoal, a thick crust of burned rice coated each cauldron. At first, just a few of us happened to be in the dining shed when the cooks scraped them clean and threw the crust on the tables. In no time at all, the word got around that the pot scrapings could be had for the asking. Dozens of kids showed up. The crust, if not badly burned, had a delicious toasted nut flavor. A bit of judicious scraping could remove the worst of the burned part. For some reason, the grownups never came to get any; they left it for the kids.

Early in December it was announced that Los Banos camp was ready to receive an additional body of internees. My best friend, Bunny, would be in that group. We said our good-byes the day before their departure.

"Will you write to me?" I asked, feeling lonely already.

"I don't know if I can send a letter from there, but I'll sure try my best," Bunny replied soberly. "We must write to each other after the war, for sure."

"How will we ever get in touch with each other?" I wondered. Suddenly I had an idea. "What if I give you my grandad's address in Kansas City? If we ever get out of here, he'll know where I am."

"That's a great idea," Bunny grinned. "When the war is over, I'll write to you in care of him. I promise."

"And I'll answer it the very same day," I sniffled. "Promise."

With hugs and a few tears we parted.

Auntie was ecstatic about going to be with her husband even though word from Los Banos indicated it was still rather primitive. "Oh, I don't care," Auntie laughed happily. "If Porter can stand it, then I can too. It's been almost six months since I saw him." Belatedly, she realized she was leaving people behind who loved her dearly. "But I'll miss all of you very much."

"Evelyn," Mother said with understanding, "your place is with Porter. I'd do the same thing if I were you."

"You'll be with Uncle Dick for Christmas," said Carole, already looking forward to the day. "Will you tell him 'Merry Christmas' for me?"

"I'm going to miss you," I said, trying not to show how much. Auntie was almost like a second mother to me. When I had yaws on my legs just a few weeks back, it had been she who bathed my legs faithfully in hot salt water. Then she sat with me to be sure I baked them in the hot sun.

While I hugged her tightly, she said in my ear, "Remember what I told you about sunset and sunrise, dear."

"My best to Porter," Dad was saying, as Auntie let me go and turned to shake his hand.

"I'll be seeing you all again someday," Auntie called as she climbed into the truck and waved. "Take care. I love all of you."

Even before Auntie left, old rumors of a shipment of Red Cross kits became concrete news, when a detail of internees was taken to the docks to unload them. First they were stored somewhere in the city; then they were brought into camp and stored in the library. Internees were becoming really anxious about whether or not the kits would ever be distributed. Finally, thirty days after the kits had arrived in Manila, we heard a commotion from our shanty.

"Come on," Dad said to us, grabbing his hat. "Let's go see what's happening."

Mother stayed with Pete, who was happily playing in his playpen, while Carole and I went with Dad to the street nearby. People were gathered around a rope barrier. They were watching some internees carry the precious kits out of the library and line them up in rows on the sunny street. Excitement among the onlookers was high. The relief kits were to be distributed at last.

A group of Japanese inspectors began hacking at the cartons with knives or swords. Their action demonstrated a singular lack of concern for the contents, which were then unceremoniously dumped on the ground. A collective gasp of disbelief went up from the crowd. The Japanese continued to wreak havoc by tearing the labels off some of the cans, even puncturing some, and confiscating all of the cigarettes. The mood of the bystanders grew ugly. It was one of the few times I ever heard Dad swear.

Behind the Japanese inspectors came the detail of internees who had placed the boxes on the pavement. They carefully, almost lovingly, restored the contents to each box as nearly as they could ascertain what went where in the mess. When the inspection was over, the boxes were left to sit in the hot sun.

Dad was seething. "If there's anything like chocolate or canned butter in those boxes, it'll melt!"

Carole looked to be nearly in tears as she said, "The ants will find out if there are any raisins."

My own anger burst out. "It's hateful of them to treat us this way," I said loudly. "And we can't do anything about it. I hate them!"

We continued to stare at the horrible scene, unwilling to leave to the elements something as valuable as those kits were to us.

"I just want to scream at them!" As I uttered those last words, Dad took my arm firmly and turned me around.

"We'd better go back to the shanty," he said. "They'll let us know when we can pick them up."

Later the same day, we were told to line up to receive the kits. Each person was given a box containing four relief kits! Our dark mood of the morning vanished in the excitement of receiving such a bonanza.

"We'll have a feast tonight, won't we, Dad?" Carole was not so much asking a question as making a statement as we lugged our precious kits to the shanty.

"You bet," said Dad with real enthusiasm. "We'll have to see what is in them first, but I'm sure we'll find something extra special for supper."

What the kits contained was almost too marvelous to comprehend all at once: chocolate, canned meat and fish, cheese, dry milk, prunes, and butter, among other things. There were a few ants in the prunes and candy, but it didn't take long to get them all off.

We ate well that night, though not extravagantly. For the next few days Dad doled out extra treats, but on a diminishing scale, until we were back to eating no more than we had before the kits came. These new kits joined, in storage, what little was left from the ones received over a year before. We tried hard to forget about the food Dad held in reserve.

I don't remember much about Christmas 1943 except that the Japanese did allow toys, made by the internees in Los Banos, to be brought to STIC. When added to the ones made in our camp, it gave each child three. To the great delight of the little kids, a Santa Claus was on hand to present the unwrapped gifts. Afterward, we older girls divided the little ones into small groups and played tag, drop-the-handkerchief, blind man's bluff, and other games with them. All of them had a good time. The very youngest were enthralled; they couldn't remember Christmas as it used to be.

Chapter 11

The internees hardly noticed the end of the old year or the beginning of 1944. Yet profound changes would soon be noticeable, as the administration of STIC passed from Japanese civilians to that of the Japanese military. About the middle of January a steady stream of orders and counterorders began to issue from the office of the new commandant, Lieutenant Konishi. If we thought life had been difficult up until then, we would shortly see how really rough it could be. Konishi, it was learned, had been a prison official in prewar Japan.

The number of guards in the camp was doubled and ordered to patrol, with fixed bayonets, among the unarmed civilian prisoners. Roll call increased from once a day to twice, regularly, and sometimes more at a moment's notice. As the officer responsible for taking the nose count and his aides passed by us, standing in rows, we were required to bow deeply in unison. If our performance was ragged or half-hearted, as it often was, we had to repeat it until the bow was deemed acceptable.

General Morimoto, head of the War Prisoners Division, made a thorough inspection of our camp. For the previous eighteen months, the Japanese had been making a small sum of money, for each internee, available to camp buyers for the purchase of food. After Morimoto's visit there would no longer be any need for camp buyers; he ordered that internees would receive the same rations the Japanese army received! The general, because he feared an increase in attempted escapes, ordered all shanties within twenty yards of the outer wall be torn down. The new empty space would have to be planted for additional garden. In accordance with that order, half-starved, emaciated men tore down the offending shanties and raised them anew far from the wall. Then began the backbreaking toil of turning the soil. No one could work at the task for more than an hour at a time, and thankfully was not required to do so more than twice a week. Understandably, the work progressed slowly, but the seed was in the ground at last.

Santo Tomas, in spite of the two major transfers to Los Banos, was continuing to grow in population; it reached four thousand strong soon after the start of the new year. The Japanese were still bringing in people who had been living in the city on temporary passes, as well as from other detention camps in and around Manila. A large group of nearly three hundred was brought up from the distant island of Mindanao. The result was extraordinary overcrowding in the buildings. The commandant was forced to allow some women and children who had shanties suitable for living to move into them. Those lucky families affected were reunited in the truest sense of the word after two full years.

In February 1944, with five days' notice, the package line was closed forever. Everyone in STIC was now completely dependent on our captors for food. Our family had not received anything through the gate for about eight months; not since Lola, due to deteriorating health, was forced to take up residence in General Hospital with Grandpa Jake. We did, however, still have a large part of our Red Cross kits intact. With apparently no thought for the future, some internees had squandered their precious foodstuff, even trading it for cigarettes. They would learn, in the months ahead, how profligate they had been.

"In a way," Dad said, one evening while he was visiting us in the annex the last hour before roll call, "we were weaned from the package line in plenty of time to begin a sound program of conservation." We were sitting on our beds, taking turns fanning Pete while he slept.

"It looks more and more as if you did the right thing by storing most of our Red Cross kits," Mother said with a meaningful look at me. "Those kits could very well mean the difference between us outlasting the Japanese or not."

It was easy, then, to see that Dad was absolutely right, but I have to admit there were times when my stomach ached terribly with hunger. At those times, I felt Dad was being mean to keep the food from us. It was almost impossible to go to sleep at night with my stomach empty and hurting.

Just two days prior to the closing of the package line, I had complained to Mother a little angrily, "I wish Dad would let us have more to eat from our boxes. I'm so hungry."

Mother laid her knitting down and raised her head to look at me. "I am too, hon." She looked so stricken, her eyes swimming in tears. "I know just how you feel," she said softly. "And I wish I could give you something to eat. But we have to believe your daddy knows best."

I was so ashamed of myself. Why hadn't I realized that Mother was hungry too? And Dad. Everyone was hungry, not just me. Hugging her tightly for several minutes, I whispered, "I wish I hadn't said anything about it." I never mentioned being hungry again.

It began to dawn on us that STIC was being systematically cut off from the outside world. Closing the package line was just one of the signs. Manila's daily newspaper was no longer distributed in camp; it had been an important window on the progress of the war. Much was learned from reading between the lines. Then, also, city trash trucks were no longer permitted to make pickups in camp; the drivers always shared what news they had with the internees. More than ever, the secret camp radio would be our last tie to the outside world.

One morning Dad came hurrying into the shanty after his shift at the camp kitchen. "Something's happening at the jail. As I was getting off work, I heard quite a ruckus coming from there or from the commandant's office." He beckoned to me and Carole. "Let's go see what it's about."

Dad was already off at a fast pace. We had to run to catch up. "Hurry," called Dad. "It might be something important."

As we rounded the front of the main building, there was a crowd of people just crossing the plaza and going toward the front gate. We three joined the quiet crowd of internees. We were all intent on finding out what the Japanese were up to. With my short stature, I can't see over any crowd, so I listened closely as Dad inquired of someone exactly what was happening up front.

"The guards have taken two men out of the jail and are taking them to the front gate," answered the man. "I don't know if they're internees or not."

"They're Filipinos," said another man close by. "It may be the two they caught stealing from a shanty last night."

"If that's who they are," the first man allowed, "it'll go hard with them. Coming over the wall to steal inside our camp shows what a hard time the people outside are having. The Japanese especially don't want those internees who have native families outside to know that. That might spark a mass breakout."

Dad's attention was diverted for the time being. Carole and I edged around to the side of the crowd so we could see ahead. The guards were pushing the two along, yelling and punching them with the butts of their guns. The natives, whose heads were covered with sacks, must have been terrified; they couldn't see where they were going or when the next blow would fall.

When the frightful scene reached the main gate, the victims were tied up near the guardhouse. Then the beatings got underway in earnest. It seemed every Japanese guard in the camp wanted his turn at beating or kicking the hapless men. The victims soon appeared to be unconscious, crumpled up on the pavement like discarded toys. If one rallied enough to move or moan, the guards descended on him again.

"Come on, girls." Dad took us by the arms. "We can't do those poor fellows any good by standing here watching." He steered us away from that horrible setting, but it did not leave my mind.

Later in the afternoon, when I could get away by myself, I felt drawn back to see how the men had fared through the heat of the day. The crowd had dwindled to only a few silent people. If the Filipinos were not already dead, I fervently hoped they were unconscious, as the guards committed one last unspeakable act. A garden hose was held over the mouth of one man so that he was actually being filled with water, like one would fill a thermos. Then, with a devilish shout of glee, a guard jumped on his stomach.

Sobbing, in a state of shock, I ran from there as fast as I could. I ran all the way to the Father's Garden. I sat down in a quiet corner, where Dr. Foley held the Protestant church services. The garden seemed to be a safe place; it offered refuge such as a real church would.

It was in this very place on Easter Sunday 1943 that Carole and I were baptized by Dr. Foley. During the peaceful and safe course of our prewar lives, Mother and Dad didn't seem to feel there was any hurry to have us baptized. Caught in the crossfire of war as we were after Pearl Harbor, they changed their minds.

Easter sunrise service was attended by many; the Father's Garden was almost full. Our baptism followed. Auntie and Uncle Dick had stood by us as Godparents. After the service, in a very meaningful way, I felt protected by Him, spiritually if not physically.

For a renewal of that comfort, I escaped to the same place following the beating at the front gate. Resting my head on the back of a pew as my sobs subsided, I drifted into a light nap. I dreamed about the many times a neighbor boy, Jack, would take me on the back of his bike to my piano lesson once a week. It was the only time I was ever allowed to leave home without our chaperon, Pascencia. Those were happy times, riding leisurely down shady streets. With my arms wrapped round Jack's waist, we would talk and laugh a lot, and always take the longest route.

The sun burning the back of my neck awakened me, to wonder why Jack and his family had not been interned with the rest of us. It must have been because they were Portuguese and Portugal was a neutral country.

One night about midnight, we were suddenly startled from our beds by the loudspeaker just outside our room. By order of the commandant, everyone was to stay in their rooms and await further orders. Babies and very young children all over the annex began crying. Everyone was up immediately, some even getting dressed, fearing we would be forced to leave at any minute. It took considerable effort, under those circumstances, to quiet the little ones. After a while, when there were no further announcements, the building gradually grew quiet once again.

"Mother," I whispered, "do you suppose something serious is happening in Dad's building?"

"I don't know, hon," she answered worriedly. "All we can do is wait until tomorrow to find out."

"When I went to the bathroom a few minutes ago, I could see lights on all over the main building," I told her. "Something is sure going on there."

"Try to go back to sleep, Georgia," she advised me. "I'm afraid we'll wake Pete up again with any more talking."

"Just wish we could see if the lights are on in the Education Building," I fumed. "I'm worried about Dad."

The next morning, over breakfast, we learned what Dad knew about it.

"Nothing happened in my building," he told us. "But from what I hear, it was bedlam in the main building from midnight until the wee small hours of the morning."

"What was it all about?" Mother wanted to know.

"Well, there must have been about a hundred guards that swarmed through the front and back entrances at the same time. They routed everyone out of their beds with all of their yelling and boot stomping." Dad paused for a bite.

"Then what happened?" prodded Carole.

"The Japanese had everyone line up in the halls while they searched every room; some of them more than once." Dad had been eating slowly, as was his habit, while Carole and I had eaten all of our mush already.

Noticing our empty bowls, Dad said, "Here, you girls finish mine. I've had enough." With that, he scraped out an equal amount for each of us. Hungry as we were, we readily accepted the extra food without really pressing Dad, as we should have, to eat his own ration.

"Thanks, Dad," I said appreciatively. "Just like the enemy to terrorize defenseless people in the middle of the night. What do you think the guards were looking for?"

"They probably thought they knew just where to look for that radio they think is hidden in the camp," Dad replied. "But they haven't found it yet!" He smiled with pleasure.

"Let's hope they never do," breathed Mother. "No telling what they would do to us if they did."

The commandant's office continued to issue new orders. The cooking oil ration was cut in half. The cakes of raw sugar, *panocha*, from which the kitchen made a syrup for our morning mush were increasingly difficult to obtain, so the sugar ration was cut. The most serious ration cut was in basic cereal grains: rice, wheat, and corn. The total was cut from 400 grams to 300 grams per person per day. This would be followed by other cuts as time went on. These orders marked the beginning of the end for many people.

Another order closed the Father's Garden to any further use of it by the internees, including for religious services. This order was received with much grumbling, as it was seen only as a means of harassing us. Practice air raid alerts, complete with blackouts, was one order that met with enthusiasm from everyone; it meant the enemy was worried, and that made us feel good.

One afternoon we all sat in the shade on the front lawn, fanning ourselves. Pete was toddling from chair to chair, making a game of getting us each to fan him. There would be another month or so of hot, dry weather. The buildings were suffocatingly hot. No breeze reached our shanty.

"Dad, why are the Japanese getting meaner and meaner?" asked Carole.

"I suspect it's because our own forces are coming nearer and posing more of a threat to their security here in the Philippines," answered Dad thoughtfully.

"Do you mean the Japanese are losing the war?" I asked, ready to accept almost any answer as a positive sign.

"Well," said Dad with hesitancy, "it won't happen tomorrow. Or even the next day. According to the latest news, the Americans haven't even landed in the Philippines yet. And if they land in the south, say on Mindanao for instance, they'll have to fight across many islands and through a lot of jungles before they reach Manila."

"But maybe they will land somewhere north of here," I remarked, growing excited at the thought. "Then, in a day or two, they could be right here in STIC." As I said it, I realized how utterly illogical it sounded. Taking back the naval base at Cavite or Clark Air Field was more important in a war than freeing a few thousand civilians. I had already lost that moment of optimism when I added, "Wouldn't that be wonderful?"

"It certainly would," Mother said happily, playing pat-a-cake with Pete. "You'd like that, wouldn't you?" she prompted him. Right on cue, he grinned and clapped his hands. Pete, in his innocence of the war, was as happy as any toddler would be in the midst of a loving family.

On Memorial Day 1944 the internees held a nondenominational service in memory of those who had died in camp since the first day of internment. The names of 249 people were read aloud to the large assembly. So many! How many more would there be before it was all over? We had not heard anything concerning Lola and Grandpa Jake for many months. We did not know if either, or both, were still living. As for Auntie and Uncle Dick, we knew they were okay because of a short note Dad handed me one day.

"Where did you get it?" I asked, interested at once as I turned the tightly folded square of dirty paper over and over. My name in pencil was just barely discernible.

"Let's just say that someone in my room gave it to me. He said it was given to him by a third party." Dad smiled mysteriously. "I don't really know how it came into camp."

"It must be from Bunny!" I exclaimed excitedly. "I'll write her one right away and maybe . . ."

"No, George." Dad frowned. "The man told me that his contact would not handle an answer. It's too dangerous."

My enthusiasm only slightly dimmed at that pronouncement, I sat down to enjoy a singular treat.

"Dear Georgia, Los Banos is all right. Our family has a room, so we can all be together, but I think STIC was better. I miss you and the long talks we used to have. I guess Pete has grown a lot. I saw your aunt and uncle this morning. They are well enough. I'm sure looking forward to a note from you. Give my regards to your family. And remember, we promised to write each other after the war. Love from your friend, Bunny."

Chapter 12

Hunger became a specter that dogged our every waking moment. Already-short rations became even shorter: rice was again cut, this time to about one cup, uncooked, a day per person. The meat or fish ration was cut until each person's portion came to less than an ounce a day. If that protein was spoiled, and it was occasionally, it was fed to the ducks with no replacement for the internees. The cooking oil allotment was down to about two tablespoonfuls per person per day. Average daily calorie intake was less than half what men with light work should have. Growing children weren't getting near enough for normal growth. In short, we were clearly starving.

News leaked to the general population that camp doctors and the internee Central Committee were discussing the use of camp reserves to bolster the dwindling food supplies provided by the Japanese. In the past, whenever possible, internee authorities had purchased canned meats and extra rice to store in the camp warehouse. The money had come largely from the Red Cross, with additional monies donated by the neutral residents in Manila. Whether or not to use those reserves now was debated all over camp. Where two or more people were gathered, the topic was bound to come up.

"The doctors are really concerned about the health of the camp children," Mother said, glancing at each of us worriedly. "You girls are so thin. Even Pete looks kind of scrawny, though I don't think he has actually been hungry like the rest of us have."

"Then what's the problem?" I wondered. "If there are reserves, and the doctors think we should use them, why aren't they being issued?"

"It's not that easy," remarked Dad. "From what I hear, if they issued the cans of corned beef, for instance, one can for every four people twice a week, it would probably only last two months. And then what—"

"That would be swell!" interrupted Carole. "Just think, we could have it chopped up with a little onion, and make a big pan of fried rice." Her face was lit up with so much enthusiasm, you'd have thought it was Christmas again.

Dad cleared his throat and said quietly, "I was about to say, then what would we do if we are still here after that is all gone?" He glanced around the table at each of us, while a heavy silence descended on the family.

Finally, Mother spoke up, "What do you think they will do, in the end?"

"We'll know what they have decided in a few days. If they begin issuing the meat now, it might improve our stamina so that we could last quite a while after it's gone." Dad paused for a minute to watch Pete throw pebbles into a mud puddle. "Or we might be able to hang on, without the extra food, a while longer the way things are, then start using the meat. They have an extremely difficult decision to make. I wouldn't want to be in their places; the well-being of four thousand people rests in their hands."

While a few of the doctors thought the time to use the reserves was not yet, the majority won out, and canned corned beef was issued as proposed. Spirits improved markedly at once. Improved health would be much slower coming.

In spite of the shadow of death from starvation hovering over the internees, morale was surprisingly good. It received an unexpected boost on June 8, 1944, when the music played for reveille that morning was "Over There." That World War I tune was chosen by the internee in charge because it meant something. Rumors flew all day about the Allied invasion on the coast of France. We heard about D-Day just two days after it happened!

After that wonderful news the most conservative estimate for our liberation was two months, before the canned goods would be depleted. Some overly optimistic people guessed we might be free in three weeks. The actions of the Japanese commandant and his guards did nothing to dispel our stubborn hope. Earlier in the year, they had brought into our camp a cow and calf, some pigs, and hundreds of ducks for their own use. They were placed in the same area where internees kept some livestock of their own. Then the Japanese commandeered from the camp garden some of our own hard-won space. They were obviously building up their own stock of survival stores, as though preparing to make a stand in the camp.

The Japanese were also fortifying STIC, not for the benefit of the internees but for the commandant and his guard. Internees, underfed as they were, were required to build two sentry towers at opposite corners of the camp. Then they were made to install large lights every twenty yards around the entire wall. These latest installations, together with the barbed wire recently strung on top of the wall, made our camp look like a prison in every way.

In spite of all these developments, Dad was still just cautiously optimistic. He was now delving only a little deeper into our reserved kits as well as from the crock of pickled duck eggs. Our general health was declining, as the doctors had noted: Mom and Dad were both suffering from gum disease and tooth loss in addition to beriberi. Though our upper bodies were quite thin, both Carole and I were beginning to experience the swelling in our feet and legs that accompanies beriberi. All of us, including Pete, were the victims of frequent bouts of dysentery.

About this time, Dad told me that he had heard of a better place for me to work. "I overheard a couple of my roommates who work at the camp hospital say they were getting better rations there than were issued on the main chow line," Dad said, studying the ground. "Maybe you ought to try to wrangle a job there, if you could." Dad seemed embarrassed to ask me to change jobs, and yet I could see he felt it would be very helpful.

"I can try, I guess. Maybe my experience at the clinic two years ago will help me out." My mind was juggling different ideas on just how to land such a catch. "I'll go tomorrow after school and see what I can do."

The next day, during visiting hours, I went to the women's ward, searching for ways to make myself useful. Fetching a glass of water for one, emptying a bedpan for another were some of the things I did that day. I went again the next day and the next. On the fourth day I got results.

"Do you work here?" asked one of the nurses.

"No, ma'am," I said, afraid my answer would cause me to be sent away. "But I'd like to," I added hurriedly.

"What's your name?" she inquired.

"Georgia, ma'am. Georgia Barnes."

"How old are you, Georgia?" she inquired skeptically.

"Fifteen my next birthday." Would I have to confess that it was still five months away?

Satisfied with that answer, she said, "Well, I could use someone as helpful as you." Pointing down the hall, she said, "That room is for the mental cases. See what you can do for them. We can't keep that one woman clothed."

Gosh! I wondered if I could handle this job, as I opened the door slightly and peeked in. There were four beds in the room, but only three were occupied. I stepped inside and shut the door. Unnoticed, I studied the patients for a while. One young woman was propped up in bed giving herself a manicure. Another, slightly older, was crooning a lullaby to a rolled towel. The third was methodically folding her clothes, one piece at a time, as she took them off.

My work at the hospital began with dressing and redressing that poor woman. The minute I turned my back, she started stripping all over again. I failed miserably in my duty one day, when she went scurrying down the hall without a stitch on. Unfortunately, one of the priests was just coming out of the chapel and collided with her. Needless to say, I was admonished to redouble my efforts.

The woman with the make-believe baby was not ever a problem unless you wanted to use the towel on her after a shower; then she cried. So I borrowed an extra towel from the linen room and hid it for just such a time. For the other patient, I tried everything I could think of to keep her from biting and picking at her fingernails and cuticles. They were a raw, bloody mess most of the time, though she didn't seem to notice the blood or feel any pain. Heavy socks tied over her hands worked for a while, until she became proficient at pulling them off with her teeth.

Three hours a day of that kind of duty was quite enough. For my efforts I received a hospital meal ticket. The first couple of months the rations there were a little bit more generous than what was served in the main kitchen. The food had to be eaten on the premises, however, so I couldn't take any of it to the shanty to share. Later, the difference was negligible.

Ignoring the Fourth of July in STIC was nearly impossible as Americans made up the majority of the camp's population. A traditional celebration with patriotic music and speeches of course was out of the question. All that was allowed in 1944 was a costume party for the young children. Afterward, the children paraded from their playhouse to the main plaza for everyone's enjoyment. The plaza was full of people enjoying the late-afternoon concert. I had gone there with my lawn chair to listen to the hour of recorded music played over the public address system. As the children marched through the crowd, it was suddenly noticed that the lead girl was carrying a small, crudely made American flag. When she passed by, people began standing up. Soon everyone on the plaza was standing at attention. It gave us all quite a thrill: the first time we had seen our flag for almost two and a half years. Luckily the Japanese were not aware of the incident.

Rumors and news, which were lifting the spirits of the internees, were having the opposite effect on our captors. It was after we learned about D-Day in France that the Japanese ordered barbed wire strung on top of the wall. When the American forces retook Guam and Saipan, the guards began digging bomb shelters for themselves inside our camp.

After a while, when the Japanese started some new project in camp, the logical question we asked each other was, "What piece of good news will we hear of next?" When the commandant ordered the entire third floor of the Education Building cleared of internees immediately, we knew something momentous had happened. Two days later we learned that the Americans had bombed Davao, the capital city of one of the large southern Philippine islands.

At the same time several Japanese ships were sunk off the coast of Tayabas, on the southern tip of the main island, Luzon. So close! No wonder the enemy was becoming nervous. They were upset enough to see the wisdom of living among the internees; quite a few of the garrison moved to the third floor of the Education Building, thereby displacing many of the men who had called those rooms home.

"That's really too bad," Mother sympathized with Dad. "You've had a nice place with a view and a breeze for over two years now."

"What are they going to do with all that space?" I asked. "It's not been very long since they moved three hundred men out of the gym and put most of them in your building."

Dad shook his head in disgust. "I don't think they know what to do, now that the tide has turned against them. The rumor is that the Japanese ambassador to the Philippines and his entire staff will be moving into our camp. That wouldn't be according to the Geneva Convention. But then, they never have followed those precepts in dealing with us as civilian prisoners of war."

"They're acting like ants in a hill that has been kicked apart," I mused. "Running this way and that, not knowing where to begin to rebuild."

"Reminds me of one of those old Keystone Cop movies," laughed Mother. "And we're going to have the last laugh!"

"Where will you go, Dad?" asked Carole.

"The room monitors haven't given us our new assignments yet. The rooms on the first and second floors are going to be awfully crowded." He frowned, studying the tin can to which he was attaching a bail. Dad had made most of our kitchen utensils from tin cans of all sizes. "They'll just have to put some of the men in the halls."

When the Japanese guards were all settled on the third floor, there were three rooms left over, so they built a barricade between their end of the hall and the other. This allowed some internees to return to the empty rooms. Dad was squeezed into a room on the first floor for a while. Then the Japanese decided to clear that floor also and turn it into a convalescent hospital. Most of those displaced men were sent back to the gym! Dad was able to stay in the Education Building on the second floor under extremely crowded conditions.

For several weeks the Japanese photographed internees in groups of five. It was a huge task, taking the picture of everyone over the age of ten, especially when it could only be done outside on a sunny day. The camera had no flash attachment, and we were in the middle of the rainy season.

Eventually they got around to the annex. It was announced over the public address system for our room to report to the photographer. Mrs. Muir, Bella, Mother, Carole, and I were in the same picture. The worst part of it was having to hold a number on our chests, just like common criminals.

"Peas," whispered Bella with a forced smile on her face.

Mrs. Muir gasped sharply.

The photographer pulled his head out from under the cloth and scowled at us. Then he grinned a humorless grin and pulled his own smile down with his fingers. It must have meant we were not to smile. Five thin, unsmiling faces were caught on film for posterity and General Morimoto of the War Prisoners Department.

One day in the first week of September, while I was on duty at Santa Catalina Hospital, a dozen or more very ill people were brought to the hospital. They were all elderly and unable to leave their beds.

"Where have they come from?" I asked the nurse next to me. Many of the staff were gathered on the stairs to see if they knew anyone among those just being admitted.

"From Philippine General Hospital," she answered casually. Then she looked at me. "Didn't you tell me your grandmother was in that hospital?"

"Yes. And my grandpa Jake too," I told her. "But they are not among these patients." The stretchers were placed helter-skelter in the lower hall until the patients could be assigned to wards upstairs. "I've already looked at every face here," I told her, disappointed. Later, I told the family about the new arrivals.

Dad was immediately interested. "Maybe one of those people could tell us something about Mother and Jake," he said hopefully. "I'll go with you tomorrow when you go to work," he told me. "You can show me who they are."

So Dad and I went together the next afternoon to question some of the patients who were well enough to talk. None of the six men we talked to knew anything about our family members. But the third lady we inquired of thought, from our description, that she had seen Lola a number of times in the hall, going to and from the shower.

"Did she seem pretty well to you?" asked Dad anxiously.

"Well, yes," the woman answered a little crossly. "Anyone who can go to the bathroom under her own power has to be fairly well off."

Patiently Dad pursued the questioning. "Did you at any time see her husband?"

"Is he a Filipino?" Not waiting for Dad's reply, she continued, "I saw her a few times with a Filipino man. He was a bigger man than the average Filipino. That's why I remember him."

"Oh, Dad," I interrupted excitedly, "that must be Jose she saw with Lola."

"Yes, I expect it was." He smiled at me. Turning back to our source of information, he told her, "That was her houseboy from prewar days. No, my mother's husband is a white-haired elderly gentleman. He's very pale because of a serious heart condition. Did you ever see anyone like that?"

"No, I'm sorry," said the lady, showing signs of fatigue. "But I did sometimes hear a male voice calling 'Yidna! Yidna!' from her room. Could that be the one you're talking about?"

"Yes," I told her happily. "That's Grandpa Jake! He always called her that in a teasing way. It means 'old woman' in Hebrew."

"So you think they are both still alive?" pressed Dad.

"I believe so. At least they were a few days ago," the lady told us.

"I can't tell you how much we appreciate hearing this news," Dad said as he rose to leave. "If there is ever anything I can do for you in return, just tell Georgia. She's here every afternoon."

"Good news, huh, Dad?" I grinned as I walked with him to the stairs.

"Certainly is," he answered with more animation than I'd seen in a long time. "And it's good to know that Jose is still helping them. He has really been a good and faithful servant. I hope we can repay him someday."

Chapter 13

Ever since March 1944 the Japanese had been calling for practice air raids, air alerts, blackouts, and fire drills. Often called at a moment's notice, they could last anywhere from one hour to four days. During such practices many of the people living in shanties took shelter in the more substantial buildings on the grounds. The resultant overcrowding made everyone irritable and impatient.

Throughout August and early September our captors must have felt the hot breath of the advancing Americans on the back of their necks; their days were spent readying themselves for imminent attack. Anti-aircraft units placed around the city practiced range-finding by firing at target sleeves pulled through the sky by planes. At other times Japanese fighter pilots put on quite an aerial display with their mock dogfights in plain view of STIC.

By mid-September the practices were more frequent and lasted so long that the camp schedule was thrown awry. Meals were either undercooked or not cooked at all. Doing without our meals, such as they were, was almost more than we as starving people could stand.

That did, however, point up a need for having some kind of food ready to eat without having to cook during an air raid. The central kitchen cooks worked out a recipe for a hardtack biscuit that very nearly defied chewing; it was thought to be impervious to weevils, as well. A thorough dunking in some of the tasteless vegetable soup, which made up such a large part of our diet, improved both the hardtack and the soup.

Soon after breakfast one bright clear day Mother asked me to take care of Pete, while she and Carole did some laundry. With a blanket and a book under one arm, I took Pete by the hand. Matching my steps to his, we walked leisurely out to the grassy expanse south of the plaza. There I settled down for two or three hours of quiet reading, while Pete played with other children nearby.

The usual Japanese aerial practice, which had begun at daylight, did not distract me from my reading. The sounds of children playing happily together assured me, without the need to look, that Pete was all right. It was not until I heard the heavy drone of many planes and some excited people yelling, "They're here! They're here!" that I looked up.

There, glistening in the dazzling sun, flew wave after wave of silver planes. One group came from the northwest, while another large formation flew toward us from the northeast. It was an impressive sight. I continued to gaze skyward, wishing devoutly they were American.

Suddenly the sky was dotted with puffs of black smoke from heavy anti-aircraft fire. Amazed by what was happening, I still did not understand the significance of it all; not until I realized people around me were grabbing their children and running for the safety of the main building. The planes must be American! The clock on the main building's tower chimed 9:30. It was September 21, 1944, and the beginning of the end. Among the last to do so, I grabbed the blanket, picked up Pete, and ran as fast as I could across the plaza. By then the sound of bombing and strafing nearby filled the air. Then, belatedly, the air raid alarm began to wail. The Japanese had been caught by surprise!

Holding Pete on my hip with one arm and clutching our things with the other, I pushed my way through the crowded hall toward the back entrance. I hoped to be able to get to the annex quickly so Mother wouldn't worry about us. It wasn't easy. The halls were jammed with people hugging and kissing each other in a frenzy of elation. The deafening excitement was exhilarating, and yet a bit frightening; I had never been witness to such a wild scene.

Standing at last by the back door, I was calculating our chances of safely making the dash to the annex, when I heard what sounded like pebbles being thrown hard upon the tin roof of the nearby dining shed.

"Young lady, you can't go out there, if that's what you're thinking," said the internee guard on duty. "That's shrapnel, or bullets, or something hitting the roof. You'll have to wait for the all-clear signal."

"Holy smoke!" I said weakly. If those were bullets, we might have been hit going out there. I turned back into the kitchen serving area. My knees trembled so much that I had to set Pete down. Just then a strong hand grasped my arm.

"Georgia, am I glad to see you," exclaimed Dad right in my ear. The uproar around us had not lessened. Picking Pete up, Dad motioned for me to follow him.

The relief I felt in Dad's company strengthened my wobbly knees. I stayed right on his heels, until we found a spot out of the main stream of traffic. Here he placed the blanket on the floor so the three of us could sit down.

"I've been searching the halls for you two," Dad said, holding Pete on his lap. "You did the right thing by coming here instead of going to the shanty," he added, patting me on the back.

"I just followed the crowd," I had to admit. "We'd have been here sooner, but for a long time I just thought it was another practice."

"Well, you're both safe now." Dad looked happier than I had seen him in years. "And I'm sure your mother and Carole are safe in the annex. Now we can enjoy the most exciting day we've had since internment."

"Is it really the Americans this time, Dad?" I wondered doubtfully.

"It really is, Georgia," he assured me. "I saw our emblem on the wing of one plane that flew very low over the camp." Dad shut his eyes for a moment, perhaps committing the sight to memory forever. Then he said, "This is a day we'll remember the rest of our lives."

"Do you think we'll be out of here soon?" I asked.

"I think it'll be all over by Christmas," Dad answered after some thought. "If not sooner."

Dad talked as if an end to our plight was nearer at hand than at any time since our internment. If Dad thought so, that was definitely a good sign.

The bombing continued off and on all day with very little respite between attacks. Many foolhardy internees stood at upper-floor windows to watch, what was for us, the renewal of hostilities. From them, word of direct hits raced through the camp population and kept us all at a fever pitch of excitement. But reports of shrapnel, empty shell casings, and even live ammunition falling within our camp kept the more timid of us hiding inside.

The next day began with a repetition of the bombing and anti-aircraft fire, which, however, ended around noon. Then for several days there were only air alerts with no activity near enough to STIC for us to be aware of it. Our spirits had quickly skyrocketed when the sounds of war, so long absent from the city of Manila, finally returned. Just as swiftly, with the planes no longer flying over our camp, our morale plummeted. We returned glumly to the mind-deadening reality of imprisonment and progressive starvation.

The 27th of September was Dad's thirty-eighth birthday. He and Carole went scrounging in the dining sheds, where the vegetable cleaning ladies were just finishing their work. They hoped to find edible scraps, which might have fallen under the tables, to add to our meager noon meal. I stayed behind in the shanty to help Mother make a birthday cake.

"This is the last of the rice flour," Mother fretted as she measured it. "Sure hope we're not still here when your birthday rolls around," she added, trying hard to smile.

"That's not for a long time yet," I reminded her. "Almost two months away. Dad told me he thinks we'll be out by Christmas or sooner." I fanned the charcoal to a red glow. "What do you think?"

"Well, I certainly hope so," Mother replied with a catch in her throat.

I looked up to see what was wrong and caught her wiping tears from her eyes. "What's the matter, Mother?" I asked, going over to put my arm around her waist. That brought forth a single sob, which distressed me all the more because I couldn't imagine what was behind it. "You don't think we'll ever get out, do you?" I whispered.

"No," she murmured, trying to gain control. "That's not it. I'm just afraid we won't get out in time."

"In time for what?" I wondered aloud, really mystified. "You're not worried about me having another birthday in camp, are you?" Trying to put real conviction in my voice, I told her, "That's not really important."

Mother took my hand and pulled me over to the table so we could sit down together. "I have something to tell you, Georgia," she said softly. She seemed to be having trouble finding the right words to use, and finally blurted out, "I'm going to have another baby."

"Oh, Mother!" I gasped. "It's such a bad time for babies." I simply refused to believe she was serious, and talked to her as though there were still time to change her mind. "I bet the Japanese wouldn't let you go outside to St. Luke's Hospital, like they did when Pete was born. Nobody gets out now for any reason."

"I know that, dear," she answered quietly, putting her arm around my shoulders. "I know, too, that you just sound cross because you're worried about me."

"Yes," I was quick to concede. Mother was more important to me than anyone else in the world, and I felt sure it was very dangerous for her to have another baby in this awful place. Planting a kiss on her cheek while hugging her tightly, I whispered, "It's not that we wouldn't all love another baby; look how much we have enjoyed Pete. I'm just afraid for you. And the baby."

"But, Georgia, our worrying isn't going to change anything," Mother reminded me. "I'm still going to have a baby. If we are liberated before it's born, though, I'm sure everything will be all right."

"When do you expect it?" I wanted to know.

"In late March," she answered.

"Oh," I sighed with relief. "The war is sure to be over long before then," I told her with certainty. "You'll see."

"Well, I feel better now that I've told you," Mother said as she rose to her feet. "We'd better get that cake in to bake pretty quick, or the charcoal will be burned up."

Knowing about Mother's pregnancy prepared me for the time I felt sick a week later and left work early. When I entered our shanty, only Dad was there. I must have caught him by surprise. He acted quite startled when I walked in just as he pulled a small bundle out of his pocket. He laid it on the table and quickly pushed it aside.

"I thought you'd be working at the hospital," Dad said quietly. I could feel his eyes willing me to not look at the bundle on the table.

"I'm supposed to be at work right now, but I don't feel well," I answered. It took a great deal of effort, but after several moments of silence, I pulled my eyes away from his. Staring at the mysterious object, I demanded, "What's wrapped up in that cloth? Food?"

Dad, looked uneasy, as though I had caught him in a crime. "Yes," he murmured, slowly unwrapping the cloth. As the last corner fell away, there was revealed a small mound of cooked rice; no more than a cupped hand could hold. "It's for your mother."

A feeling of relief swept over me, as I knew immediately that Dad really intended the extra food for her, and not himself. "I guess Mother needs it more right now than any of us," I said, ashamed of the way my stomach was growling.

"I'd bring some for all of you if I could." Dad's voice begged my understanding. "You know that, don't you?"

I nodded my head. I believed him implicitly and understood why he always insisted on having a clean handkerchief to take to work.

"Let's not let this secret go any further, George," Dad said, rewrapping the rice and setting a can over the bundle to protect it from flies. "It's risky business."

"You can count on me." Sitting down and resting my head on the table, I mumbled, "I feel awful, Dad."

He felt my forehead and declared me feverish. When I complained of aching all over, he'd heard enough. Dad promptly took me to the hospital, where Dr. Fletcher pronounced it a case of flu. I was put to bed, where I enjoyed three days of rest.

During the first half of October the Japanese worked furiously, sometimes far into the night, bringing stores of various kinds into our camp. They put up three large tents in front of the Education Building first, and then proceeded to fill them. A conservative guess by internee officials now placed the number of Japanese soldiers in our camp at six hundred; far more than was needed to keep us from escaping.

To add to the general turmoil in camp, the garrison that had occupied the third floor of the Education Building just two months earlier moved down to the first floor. This forced a complete reshuffling of everyone in the building. The convalescent patients were moved up to the second floor, while the men bunking there moved to the third. Dad was back in his old room. The addled Japanese were in confusion, resulting in considerable chaos for the weary and long-suffering internees.

Following two days of intense bombing, the Japanese did an about-face. They began hauling out of our camp all the material they had just spent two weeks bringing in. It was not long afterward that we learned their frenetic activities were due to a major advance by the Americans. General Douglas MacArthur's forces had landed on the island of Leyte! The general had kept his word about returning. It was the first such landing in the Philippines, and naturally sent the internees into moderate expressions of delight.

As October, with its rains and high winds, drew to a dripping, muddy close, the number of dead for the month came to nine. The two-month supply of canned meat had been doled out until there was no more. The death toll would grow more rapidly as a result. Our captors had not brought in any rice or corn for the entire month. STIC's own reserves of those vital cereal grains were down to a two-week supply.

Starving to death is a slow process. The victims, one meager meal at a time, turn into listless skeletons. When white screens went up around a bed in the hospital, I knew another luckless patient was not going to make it to the liberation we all prayed for. For many there was little hope if we had to wait much longer.

November began much as October had for us: being confined to our quarters much of every day because of either air alerts or actual raids. Mere alerts allowed us to sink deeper and deeper into depression. Real air raids were vastly more interesting, as we sat for hours on end in our respective buildings speculating on what had been hit or from where the smoke was coming. For our morale to rise very much during these hard times, it required a really heavy bombing, fires ringing the city, and explosions in the bay area. Best of all was seeing Japanese planes shot down.

By the middle of November, camp rice reserves were gone. Henceforth we would get only what the Japanese gave us. At that time the ration they issued was less than one cup a day of uncooked rice for each person twelve years of age and up. Children under that age received half rations. To put on our morning mush, there was a quarter cup of very watery coconut milk. By the end of November, even that was taken away. At night we were served a half cup of thin vegetable soup with our rice. No midday meal was issued through the central kitchen for two reasons: no food and very little fuel with which to cook it.

Dad and Mother still tried to fix us something to eat at noon. If there was an air raid in progress, Dad would sneak out to the shanty by himself to prepare it. We waited anxiously for him to return, because we knew that many times he had to take cover under a neighbor's shack when shrapnel started flying around.

Our family reserves were running very low. The duck eggs were all gone. All that was left of the Red Cross kits were eight cans of corned beef, one can of Prem, and six cans of evaporated milk. Naturally, there were a great many rumors concerning possible distribution of more kits. They should come any time, the rumor went. Hadn't it been just about a year since we got our last ones?

Our preoccupation with the subject of food carried through to my fifteenth birthday. The 23rd of November coincided with Thanksgiving that year, the best we could calculate, so the folks tried especially hard to fix a nice meal. The last typhoon had blown down a banana tree near our shanty. Dad cut a two-inch-diameter section out of the heart of it to slice and boil. The last can of Prem, thinly sliced and browned in a skillet, graced our table.

"Even though the banana tree heart doesn't really taste like much of anything," Mother said with a poignant smile, "you can imagine it's mashed potatoes."

"Well," said Carole doubtfully, "it's the right color." Chewing the fibrous vegetable for a while, she swallowed and said with a funny little grin, "I guess I don't know how to imagine hard enough."

I ate mine as quickly as I could. Then, cutting the Prem in very tiny pieces, I chewed them as long as I could make it last, to keep the delicious flavor in my mouth. It tasted like baked ham. Looking at Mother fondly, I mused, "I remember you always fixed what I wanted for my birthday."

"And you always asked for roast leg of lamb," put in Mother. "It did make a scrumptious meal."

"This is almost as good," I assured her.

"Wait until dessert time!" Carole exclaimed animatedly. "It's the best goodie we've had in a long time."

And so it was. Little rice fritters, each about the size of an American dollar, fried golden brown. They were slightly sweet. "They taste lovely!" I marveled. "But there's something different about them. I don't know what."

Mother giggled. "We fried them in the last of my Pond's cold cream. That's why they have such a pretty scent."

December was worse than November. Every day children had to be ordered away from the Japanese cook house. They were begging for food! In addition to this insensitivity to the children's condition, many acts of inhumane treatment and even cruelty were visited upon the adults in camp. Our captors literally had their backs against the wall. They lashed out at us with beatings for some, demands for increased labor from everyone, and harassed all of us with repeated, lengthy searches of every building in the camp. Their actions told us, louder than words could have, that they feared the eventual outcome of the war.

For over two weeks there was no bombing of Manila. We almost gave up looking for the planes on whose silver wings our hopes flew. By the middle of December they came back. Instead of the smaller carrier-based planes, they were the big B-29s. Land-based planes meant the Americans were closer. With the bombers came the beautiful twin-tailed fighters called P-38s. A few internees were caught watching the magnificent display and were severely beaten.

For three days and nights they pounded every military objective in and around Manila. After that there was very little resistance left, practically no ack-ack fire, and there were few Japanese fighter planes to challenge the Americans. The general feeling among the internees was that this latest, most concerted attack could only be the forerunner of imminent liberation. Then followed a period of infrequent appearances of American planes. Despair crept back into our hearts. News of the recent landing on the island of Mindoro buoyed our hearts only briefly. We had been waiting for deliverance almost three years.

Another drastic cut in the rice ration was offset by the addition of what the commandant said was soybean refuse. Our own officials recognized it for what it was: cattle feed. Added to our diet, it gave us a little bulk and some much-needed protein. That helped us through the realization that there would be no Red Cross kits this year.

The prospect of yet another Yuletide season behind prison walls was unthinkable, and yet it was almost upon us. A few days before Christmas, the Japanese created such a stir by throwing four internees into jail that virtually all thought of the holiday left us.

"Many others have been jailed these last three years, and you weren't this upset," I said to Dad. "Who are they?"

"I know two of them: Carroll Grinnell and Alfred Duggleby," Dad answered with deep concern.

"Oh, my gosh!" My heart sank, and I knew why Dad was so disturbed. "Those two are the best men in the whole camp."

"Absolutely," he agreed. "They have worked tirelessly and selflessly on the Internee Committee. They have fought a battle of wits with the Japanese ever since we were interned here. If it were not for Grinnell and Duggleby and the rest of the committee, we could not have survived this long."

"Why were they arrested?" I asked.

"No one knows for sure," Dad answered glumly. "But the situation doesn't bode well for them, or for us." He stared blankly at the ground.

The most memorable event of the holiday season 1944 was the greetings sent us by the US Army. We awoke Christmas morning to find a number of leaflets had been dropped over our camp during the night. The wishes for a merry Christmas and the realization of our fervent hopes for the New Year meant a great deal to us. The kitchen doled out two spoonfuls of jam and a small piece of chocolate for every internee. A short Christmas program was permitted, but there were no presents for the children. Listless and weak, we could hardly remember how it used to be.

One evening after supper, Carole hurried into the shanty out of breath. "Hurry," she said in a stage whisper. "The kitchen is giving away seconds. The line is already around to this side of the main building."

I grabbed a can and made a wild dash out to the street, where I joined the rapidly growing line. Carole and Dad were right behind me.

After a while, Carole commented, "The line isn't moving. I wonder what the holdup is."

"Are you sure you heard right?" Dad questioned her.

"Yes. I heard someone say there was an extra pot of food left from supper," she answered, then added defensively, "I'm not the only one who heard it."

That was certainly true enough. The end of the line was out of sight. Then the PA system came on. "We are sorry to have to inform you that an erroneous rumor was started concerning seconds on the chow line. There is no more food to be issued. Again, we're sorry."

Chapter 14

Japanese officers and men in our camp, in spite of having nothing at all to celebrate, were nevertheless roaring drunk by noon on New Year's Day 1945. Internees, waiting with stoic calm for the liberation we felt sure was near, doggedly hung on to life with our fingernails. To mark the end of our third year in captivity, it was announced that the holiday vacation from school would be extended indefinitely. Everyone, teachers and students alike, was happy to hear that; no one had the strength any longer to climb the stairs to the fourth floor.

Another major shuffle in the Education Building in December had taken the convalescent patients from there to the gym. That opened up the entire second floor for occupancy. To no one's surprise, more Japanese moved into our camp and filled all that space. Those high-ranking civilian and military officials brought with them thirty trucks loaded with their baggage and furniture. Much of the latter was obviously antique and part of the Philippine national treasure. Despite the noisy occupants on the lower two floors of the Education Building, Dad was still content to be in his old third-floor room.

The Internee Committee tried a number of times to win the release from jail of their fellow members Grinnell and Duggleby, to no avail. The jailers would not even permit anyone in camp to communicate with them. After two weeks the men were whisked out of camp and taken no one knew where.

"Why, Dad?" I felt, as did everyone else in camp, that our situation could only worsen with them gone.

"Rumor says that a broadcast from San Francisco indicated that our present condition here in camp is well known to the American authorities," Dad began. "The Japanese probably feel sure that such information was somehow relayed by our committee members. I fear for their lives since they have been taken out of camp."

Although the fate of those men concerned us, our minds were more occupied with events that had begun to move more rapidly since the start of the new year. The Japanese were seen to be burning some of their records. They vacillated between demanding more bowing on the one hand and being so wrapped up in their own fears that they didn't return the courtesy when we did bow. Air raids occurred night and day, sometimes lasting a whole week at a time.

I'll never forget one special day. It was January 11. Dad, Carole, and I were outside getting some fresh air; there had been no planes overhead for an hour or so. Suddenly a roar, which grew louder every second, caused us to look up in time to see two planes flying at treetop level toward us. At first I couldn't tell if they were enemy planes about to strafe us or if they were American, but my fear grew until I was about to flee, when I saw the white star in a blue circle on the wings. "It's ours!" I yelled. "Look! He's waving at us!"

Everyone outside began waving and cheering as the two planes, wagging their wings, disappeared over the main building. It was hard to believe that people who moments before were so listless could then act so exuberant.

Later, over a lunch of thin, watery rice, Carole commented with a grin, "Did you see the first pilot? He pulled his sunglasses off. I could almost see the color of his eyes."

"I think the Americans rule the skies now," said Mother happily. "They must be coming very close."

"I would say so," agreed Dad with intensity. "I heard a wonderful rumor just this morning about . . ."

"What was it, Dad?" I pressed excitedly. "Tell us." Glancing at me with an understanding smile, he continued. "I heard that the American forces have made landings at Lingayen Gulf in the north and at Batangas in the south."

"Really!" we all exclaimed together. Our high spirits must have been catching; Pete started kicking his feet against his chair and clapping his hands.

With this good news, we were heartened to see the city shrouded in smoke by day and ablaze with fires by night. Much of the destruction going on around us was caused by the bombings, but increasingly it was from demolition by the Japanese. Just as the same scene had signaled the pullout of the Americans three years before, it now meant the Japanese were losing the battle for Manila. They were preparing to abandon the city.

A few days later rumors placed our forces at the town of Angeles, only about fifty-five miles north of Manila. Every night Dad had a ringside seat at his third-floor window to watch the bright flashes of gunfire in the sky. Camp buildings would growl with the low-level vibrations of explosions.

On the 16th of January a man by the name of Eisenberg escaped from camp. This event, enjoyed by all internees, threw the enemy into a highly nervous state. They threatened thereafter to shoot anyone seen within twenty yards of the wall.

We learned later that this man's daring escape had a great deal to do with the US Army's accelerated attempt to reach us.

A few nights later the Japanese in the Education Building could be heard taking part in some kind of ceremony, at which they all swore an oath. Afterward the enemy kept the internees above them awake far into the night with their drunken carousing. Three days later they spent several hours going through a bayonet practice in full view of the camp. It was clear to everyone in STIC that the Japanese knew the end was near. And yet the last day of January found us still waiting.

For some, unfortunately, the waiting had gone on too long. In November we lost twelve souls to illness and starvation. For December the death toll was seventeen. It was especially sad that these sick and weakened people had endured so much for so long only to die just as our hope was about to be realized. By the end of January we had seen the bodies of thirty-two more internees taken away.

On Thursday, February 1, the Japanese slaughtered an ox they had kept in our camp, for a feast. The starving camp children watched in silent envy; many of them carried a can or bucket in case there might be some scrap dropped carelessly in the dirt or thrown away. About fifty pounds of the carcass, mostly bone, was given to the camp kitchen for four thousand people.

The next day enemy soldiers busied themselves burning still more records. They butchered the remaining oxen and hogs, but did not share any of that meat with the camp. Then they stripped the camp garden of everything edible they could find. Next, they emptied their own warehouse of all foodstuffs, hauling it out of camp. Even some of our own rice reserves were taken. Internees felt sure the Japanese themselves would be the next to leave. But they stayed.

All that night shelling could be heard to the north and east. Fires ringed the city; the smoke was thick enough to choke us. Sometime during the night a huge explosion set me bolt upright in bed. It was a long, unrestful night that finally ended with the sunrise on Saturday, February 3, 1945.

There was no bombing that day, although explosions from demolition occurred periodically. I thought the city must be in complete ruins. I wondered what had happened to all the people outside. Was anyone still alive out there? Santo Tomas, of course, had been spared from bombing by the Americans. The Japanese would not blow up one of their prime refuges. Other than a stray shell that crashed through the ceiling in one of the upper rooms of the Education Building there was no damage or accidental loss of life, thus far, in our camp.

After supper late Saturday afternoon several American planes flew very low over the camp and were wildly cheered by internees watching the flyover. As we watched, something either fell or was thrown from one of the planes. It was a pair of pilot's goggles with a piece of paper stuck in them. The message read, "Roll out the barrel!"

"What could that mean?" I questioned Dad.

"Well, as you know, the next line of that song is 'We'll have a barrel of fun,'" said Dad. "The exact meaning isn't clear to me right now."

"But it's a positive message, don't you think?" queried Mother as she went about the shanty setting things to rights for the night. We were almost ready to go to our rooms. It would soon be sunset and time for roll call.

"Good night, Dad," I said as I took Pete by the hand for the short walk. "We'll see you in the morning."

We started on ahead, while Mother tarried a moment longer. I heard her caution Dad about getting some rest instead of staying up half the night to watch the firepower display on the battlefields around the city.

When we reached the annex, we learned there would be no roll call; the Japanese were in such a dither, they didn't know which way to turn. At any rate they were much too busy with their own affairs to conduct a nose count. That certainly was a good omen. Add to that the sound of machine-gun fire in the near distance, and you could almost smell freedom. I let my imagination run wild in the last few minutes of twilight. At 7:30 p.m. the camp experienced a power failure, which knocked out the public address system as well as the lights. Mother put Pete to bed, but even singing didn't soothe him to sleep. There was such a growing sense of expectancy among the inmates of the annex that small children could feel it.

"Mother," whispered Carole plaintively, "I don't think I could go to sleep right now. Can we stay up a little while longer?"

"I guess so," replied Mother softly. "Everyone seems awfully keyed up for some reason."

"I think I'll go out and sit on the front steps for a while," I told Mother. "The Japanese won't see us in the dark tonight."

In an attempt to quiet us, Mother said, "Go ahead. But you girls stay together. And don't leave the building."

We quickly darted from the room for fear she would change her mind. We groped our way out to the front of the annex, where we found a sizable crowd of people already gathered. The several groups were talking in whispers among themselves of the day's events. Sounds of occasional bursts of gunfire seemed to be drawing closer to our camp. There were no other sounds of life either in the camp or outside the walls. It seemed to me that the whole world had come to a complete stop and was waiting, with its breath held, for something important to happen.

We hadn't been outside more than thirty minutes when everyone fell silent, listening intently to the heavy rumbling sound coming from somewhere on the other side of the camp's western wall.

"That kinda sounds like tanks," said a masculine voice.

"Are they Japanese tanks?" asked a faceless woman.

"Hard to say," answered the man. "Just have to wait and see. It could be the enemy planning to take up positions around our camp."

"My God!" gasped another woman. "Are they going to fight a battle right here?"

"Oh, I don't think so," put in a different man. "I heard a rumor just minutes ago that the commandant and his staff left by car a little while ago. The rest of the garrison will probably surrender meekly when the Americans get here."

Carole and I stood at the fringes of the small group, taking in every word. Speculative talk went on for another half hour while the crowd continued to grow. A new rumor circulated to the effect that the commandant had returned to camp only minutes after leaving. Tension was doubling and redoubling by the minute. People, no longer bothering to whisper, were talking loudly and excitedly. Where were all the guards? Why hadn't they rushed us with their bayonets and ordered us back into the building?

The camp was now totally dark, as the tower clock tolled nine. Suddenly there was the rapid fire of machine guns, surely no farther than the front wall! Some in the crowd began running toward the south end of the annex.

"Come on, Carole. Let's go too," I urged her. "Something really big is happening!"

Holding hands so we could stay together in the dark, we followed the rest. The crowd bunched up in the street between the annex and the main building. Machine-gun and rifle fire kept up an incessant racket. Just then it looked like a giant lightbulb had been turned on above the camp.

"Flares!" shouted someone.

At the same time we could hear a deafening crash of metal on metal. It echoed through the camp, followed by the rumble and creak of tanks. I didn't think Japanese tanks would crash through their own gate. Our uncertain group, still unable to see what was happening at the main gate, inched nervously toward the front of the main building.

"Oh!" everyone gasped and froze in mid step. A tank had turned the corner and was sweeping the street with its searchlight. In spite of the blinding light, there was a mad scramble to get out of the way of the tank's cannon as it swung back and forth seeking a target. Hugging the side of the building, we watched anxiously as the tank came to a ponderous stop just in front of us.

The hatch opened. A soldier stood up, holding his gun at the ready. A dim light from inside the tank cast grotesque shadows on his face. His mouth moved as though he were speaking, but we could hear nothing except the tank engine. After a moment's thought I shouted in Carole's ear, "The Japanese don't chew gum! That's a Yank!"

Another soldier walked out of the shadows behind the tank into the searchlight. In a distinctly American voice he said, "Hello, folks!"

Pandemonium broke loose. People went crazy, crying and laughing at the same time. The foot soldier had trouble keeping his feet on the ground; internee men wanted to carry him on their shoulders. The tank crew warned the delirious crowd to take cover inside the building until the enemy was rounded up and the camp secure. They were finally able to continue their search. Carole and I ran back to the annex to spread the good news.

"Mother, we're free!" Carole was yelling as we entered the room.

Mother was dressing Pete, who looked around confused in the dim glow of a single candle. "Dad should be coming soon," Mother told us confidently.

"Mother, can we go to the main building for just a little while?" I begged. "There must be quite a celebration going on there by now."

"I'd like for you to stay here until your father comes." She spoke hesitantly, unsure of exactly what we ought to do under these new and wonderful circumstances.

"Please, Mother," I pressed. "We're missing all the excitement!"

Looking doubtfully at us, she finally agreed. "Just for a little while now, girls."

Running happily, we left the annex and found we were not alone. The streets were full of exuberant and rejoicing internees going in every direction. We entered the rear entrance of the main building, where a crush of people was wildly congratulating each other at the top of their voices. It was impossible to get through. Thinking it would be easier to get to the front door and main lobby by going around the east side of the building, we headed in that direction as fast as we could go.

"Halt!" cried a soldier from the corner of the building. "Where are you girls going?" he demanded.

Frightened, we stood still while a light was shone in our faces. "We just want to get around to the front of the building," I answered. "We want to join the celebration."

"Well, you'll have to go around the other side," he told us more gently. "This street has been closed off because the Japs are holed up in that building over there."

"In the Education Building?" Carole asked worriedly.

"Whatever it's called." He shrugged his shoulders. "It's that three-story one over there."

"Where are the men who were housed there?" I questioned him nervously. "Our father lives in that building."

"Nobody has come out of there yet. The Japs are holding them all hostage," he said. Pointing in the opposite direction, he added, "Go around that way. You might learn something about your dad in the main lobby. That's where the First Cavalry has set up headquarters."

Hardly waiting for him to finish, we went the other way. No one barred our path. Soon we were in the noisy crowd of internees on the front plaza. As we pushed and shoved our way to the front door, a shot rang out nearby. A loud cheer filled the air as we caught a glimpse of a Japanese officer lying on the ground.

It was Abiko, the officer who had drilled us relentlessly in the proper way to bow. The word was, he was acting as one of the envoys between the Japanese commandant and the American major in charge. A Yank thought he was making a move for a hand grenade. He shot him on the spot. Mortally wounded, the horrid man was dragged by his heels through a crowd that showed him no mercy. Kicked and spat upon, he was pulled into a clinic where he died a few hours later in spite of first-aid treatment.

We squeezed ourselves into the tightly packed lobby along with hundreds of other insanely happy internees. A few weary Yanks stood at the door. Never before that time nor since have I experienced such a towering and lasting level of pure happiness. It was euphoria lifted to the mountaintop. No smile could ever be big enough to express it. A profound feeling of thankfulness filled my eyes with tears. My heart could barely hold such a mix of emotions.

"Your attention please! Folks!" An American officer standing on a table was gradually able to quiet the crowd.

"We have just learned that the Japs in the Education Building refuse to surrender." Looking around at the people beneath him, he waited for that news to be digested. "They have also refused to release the two hundred internees trapped on the upper floors."

The officer had gained the attention of all but the most determined celebrants. "We are going to have to persuade the Japs to give up. We'll do it with the welfare of those hostages in mind. If we can. For your own safety, stay away from there." He leaped from his podium and went straight to the task at hand.

"We'd better go tell Mother what's happening," Carole said, tugging at my arm.

"You go," I told her. "I'll be right here when you get back. Maybe I'll know something new by then."

With a promise to return soon, she left reluctantly. The noisy celebrating had resumed except for a group of sober-faced individuals gathered at the main entrance. I thought they might be relatives of the hostages, so I joined the group. We didn't stay at the entrance long but moved outside, toward the Education Building. No military challenge slowed our progress, until we stood with the terrifying scene before us. Four tanks had taken positions in front of the building. Then a warning was shouted to the hostages to take cover. Some long minutes passed; then at a signal the tanks fired their cannons at the first floor. Soldiers raked the lower windows with rifle and machine-gun fire. It seemed to me that no one, friend or foe, could survive the wrath of the army's might. My fear for Dad nearly smothered me.

After a few minutes the firing ceased. When asked if they were now ready to surrender, the Japanese again refused. A second barrage was ordered with no better results. Clearly the presence of the internees in the building was hampering efforts to rout the Japanese. Further negotiations failed to alter the standoff.

Carole rejoined me with the news that Mother had once again put Pete to bed. "She's worried sick about Dad," she told me. "She wants both of us to come back pretty soon so we can wait together for him to be freed."

But the situation was so electric, I was unable to force myself to leave. "We'll go in a little while," I assured her. "They'll let Dad and the others out soon."

"I'm going to stay too," she said. "For a while."

Sometime after midnight the American major sent a message to the hostages for everyone to go to bed; there would be no more shooting or bargaining until daylight.

The highly excitable state of nervous tension I had been in since sunset had at last become untenable. An overwhelming weariness swept over me. I must have been in shock. My legs were leaden. My body shivered. "Come on, Carole," I mumbled from between chattering teeth. "Let's go." We walked woodenly through the still-exulting throngs back to our room.

Mother's welcoming hug was very intense. She must have been worried about us. When we told her that it didn't look as though Dad would be released before morning, she said, "Then it will do no good for us to wear ourselves out tonight." She put us to bed as if we were Pete's age.

I fell asleep immediately, but tossed and turned a lot. I dreamed someone was trying to wake me. I told them to leave me alone; I was too tired to get up.

"I know how tired you are, hon," said Mother as she shook my shoulder again. "But I want you to know that your father is safe now."

"Dad?" I mumbled. "Did he get out?"

"See for yourself," Mother told me. "He's sitting right there on my bed."

And he really was. I could just make out his face in the dawn's first light. "Dad! How did you get out?"

"It's a long story. I'll tell you all about it later," whispered Dad, trying not to wake Pete.

"Dad? Is that you, Dad?" asked Carole sleepily.

"Yes," he said with a tired smile. "You girls go back to sleep now. Everything is going to be all right."

Chapter 15

The first day free of Japanese domination started just as we would have wished: breakfast was a good thick mush with seconds available. Our camp cooks must have cooked a regular three- or four-day ration. What a good feeling it was to have a full stomach! We couldn't eat in our shanty because of its proximity to the Education Building, where the hostage stalemate continued, so we joined the lively crowd in the dining sheds.

"Now tell us how you got out last night, Dad." Carole asked the question uppermost in our minds.

"Well," Dad began between bites, "after the tanks fired their second barrage and the Japanese still would not surrender, it looked more and more like an extremely dangerous situation for the hostages. So some of the men in my room began to plan an escape."

"What did you do?" I interrupted, hardly giving Dad an opportunity to eat.

"We tied enough sheets together to almost reach the ground from the third floor. Then we tied it to the transom over the door and dropped it out the window. That drew a burst of gunfire."

"The Japanese are really trigger-happy if they're firing at a sheet rope," commented Mother.

"We finally realized it was the Americans shooting at the first-floor windows. I guess they could see what we were planning to do. Actually, they were helping us by keeping the Japanese away from the windows," Dad told us. "Anyway, when we knew it wasn't the enemy shooting at us, we started down the makeshift rope."

"Were you the first to go?" I prodded. "How many escaped like that?"

"I wasn't the first or the last. I really don't know how many got out," he said thoughtfully. "But some were hurt. The man below me took a stray bullet in the leg.

I was almost all the way down when the elderly man above me lost his grip and fell, knocking me to the ground. Luckily I wasn't hurt; I jumped up and ran for cover."

The rest of the hostages had to wait another twenty-four hours for their freedom. The stalemate was finally settled by negotiation. The commandant and his guards were disarmed and escorted out of the camp to a place they chose, where they were left to their own devices.

In the meantime, men of the First Cavalry, our liberators, were setting up their pup tents, a first-aid station, and a mess tent. They were also digging foxholes.

"Since they're digging foxholes," Mother reasoned, "it sounds like they expect the Japanese to attack." We were gathered in our shanty, once again able to enjoy the use of it now that the enemy was gone from camp.

"Oh, I don't really think that's the case," answered Dad with confidence as he helped Mother set the table. "The officers just like to keep their men busy when they're not actually in battle."

"You know what I heard today?" Not waiting for an answer, I told the family, "I heard there were only two hundred men and just five tanks that came to rescue us Saturday night. How could so few have done that?" I marveled.

"It was a very daring feat," Dad addressed us all. "If the Japanese had known that, the outcome could very well have been quite different—our liberation delayed."

"Why didn't a bigger army come?" asked Carole.

"The way I heard it," said Dad, sitting down, "was like this: Remember back in January there was a man by the name of Eisenberg who escaped? It turns out he was able to reach the American lines to the south and tell them that few of us would survive if rescue did not come soon. So the First Cavalry was chosen to make the mission of mercy."

"What does 'flying column' mean?" I questioned. "I heard the First Cavalry called that."

"It means a group that is sent out ahead of the main force to make a spearhead drive toward an objective," explained Dad. "The advantage of such a maneuver is speed and surprise."

"It could also mean," put in Mother, "that if things go wrong, such a small group of men could be outnumbered by the enemy and wiped out. We're very fortunate that it worked."

"Of course," Dad went on, "reinforcements of men and tanks continued to come in all that night. In fact I believe reinforcements are still arriving."

"Yeah," Carole agreed. "The front lawn looks like a regular army camp. They're even setting up gun emplacements."

Those first few days of the American reoccupation were busy ones for the internees as well as the army. Every person and family was registered according to their nationality so that plans for sending us home could begin. The army brought in their field hospital along with a corps of nurses. The two lower floors of the

Education Building were cleared of rubble; it was there the army set up their hospital for ailing internees as well as wounded soldiers.

Monday morning, after the Japanese garrison had been marched away, someone produced an American flag. While it was being attached to the short pole overhanging the entrance to the main building, people began singing "God Bless America." Because the loudspeaker was still not working, there were only a few people present at first. As the crowd grew, the singing swelled, until still more people were drawn to the site. Internees leaned from the open windows to join in. Soldiers wandered over from their bivouac to become a part of the impromptu gathering. It was an emotion-filled scene, which I shall never forget. Everyone was dabbing at tears.

On Wednesday, February 7, Santo Tomas was expecting a visit from General Douglas MacArthur. A crowd gathered early, but had to take shelter when several enemy shells landed within the camp. After a while the honor guard regrouped and internees once again ventured outside.

Suddenly a tall lanky figure with a corncob pipe clamped between his teeth appeared among us. He greeted old friends, shook hands with the officers, then mounted the stairs in the main lobby. Halfway up the stairway he turned to wave at the crowd. Cheering echoed off the walls. General MacArthur made a brief speech, which concluded with the phrase "I have returned." That set off thunderous cheers again.

Although he was gone as quickly as he had come, the momentous event left us internees feeling more like human beings than we had in three years. To have merited a visit from such a busy, important person was something to talk about. A five-star general, he was Supreme Commander of the Pacific Forces.

Later that day a convoy of trucks entered the camp loaded with army rations, enough to feed everyone. Tankers of potable water were placed at convenient sites around camp, complete with paper drinking cups. Dad and the other camp cooks were furloughed when a crew of Chinese cooks, drawn from the city's population, was brought in to take over the cooking. We were overwhelmed with the sudden plenty everywhere in evidence, as well as with the way in which the American troops were taking care of us.

The abundant army food caused problems for many; unused as we were to much except watery rice, the army rations proved to be too rich. Hundreds were made ill at first. The army learned that starving people must be reintroduced gradually to ordinary food. For others, the food came too late. Deaths for the first five days of the month came to nine. At that rate, the number might easily have reached sixty for February had liberation not come when it did.

Since liberation on February 3, there had been a few Japanese shells land within the camp, causing some damage but no loss of life. American soldiers had shot some snipers who were firing into our camp from roofs outside the camp. American tanks had lumbered out of the gate on several seek-and-destroy missions. For the most part, however, internees took very little notice of such happenings. We were only vaguely aware that the enemy, making a stand on the south bank of the Pasig River, was methodically destroying Manila. Then, without warning, STIC caught the full brunt of a war not yet over. In the afternoon following the general's visit our camp was deliberately shelled by the Japanese, who showed no mercy for the thousands of innocent noncombatants still housed there. Terror struck at our hearts, as great gaping holes were blown in every building. No safe place could be found. The room where we had first lived, three years earlier, received a direct hit. The Education Building, already pockmarked with shell holes, sustained many more hits. Even the annex was shelled.

That terrible day saw twelve internees die; twelve who had just begun to live again. Dozens were wounded. The death of Dr. Foley, the minister of our church, was the hardest for our family to take. Mrs. Foley was severely wounded. In addition, two soldiers and eight hired workers were killed. Over the next three days four more internees and two hired workers were killed.

Most internees came through those dark days physically unscathed, but mentally, many of us suffered from shell shock. The American artillery was set up some distance north of Santo Tomas, but fired over us to reach the Japanese entrenched to the south. The constant firing and detonations did not let up for days. We were helplessly caught in the crossfire of two armies battling for domination.

Fighting was intense all over the city. American troops did not reach Philippine General Hospital, where some Japanese had taken refuge, until about two weeks after Santo Tomas was freed. During efforts to dislodge the enemy, Grandpa Jake and Lola sought safety in the shallow crawlspace under the hospital. It was from this terrifying final phase of captivity that they were rescued. It is almost beyond belief that they survived. It was not surprising that they would not ever talk about it to me. Manila was not cleared of Japanese until late February.

On the 23rd of February, most of the camp attended burial services for Carroll Grinnell, A. F. Duggleby, and two other internees who had been executed by the Japanese. Their bodies, all apparently beheaded, had been found in a vacant lot near the Philippine General Hospital. Fellow internees had long wondered about the fate of the four. With their remains decently laid to rest in the Father's Garden, bitterness over their fate filled us all.

Walking back to our shanty after the funeral, Mother expressed the sadness we all felt, when she said angrily, "There was absolutely no reason for those men to have been killed. They were good men who did everything they could to improve our lives as prisoners."

"It won't bring them back," said Dad, "but it helps a little to know that there probably isn't one of the murderers who is alive today."

Out of the hot sun and into the relative coolness of our shanty, we sat down to rest. Mother was feeling more energetic since our diet had undergone an immense improvement, but being quite large with child, she still needed frequent rests. She sat fanning herself, while I gave Pete a drink of water. Carole took one to Mother.

"Now that we're all together," began Dad, "I can tell you the good news I heard just before the funeral." Looking at each of us to be sure he had our attention, he said, "Los Banos camp was liberated this morning!"

"Thank the Lord," breathed Mother. "Are Evelyn and Porter safe?"

"They must be. There was no loss of life among the internees during the military action," he assured us.

"Was it the First Cavalry Division and their tanks that freed them?" I asked, anxious to know the details.

"No," said Dad with an air of amazement. "If it was anything at all, it was even more exciting and daring than was our own rescue."

"We're dying to know all about it, Dad." I tried to hurry the story along. "Who rescued them?"

"It was a combined effort. First came the paratroopers, aided by guerrillas. Then came the amtracs."

"What in the world are amtracs?" asked Carole.

"Sheldon," interrupted Mother, not understanding the sequence of events, "start from the beginning."

"It seems the internees were lined up for morning roll call at 7:00 a.m. as usual. All of a sudden they looked up to see paratroopers floating down. They landed very near the camp. The Japanese guard at the gate had already been killed by guerrillas. The rest of the garrison were quickly dispatched as well."

"What a sight that must have been!" I commented.

Dad continued, not needing encouragement now. "The commander in charge of the rescue told the internees they had just a few minutes to get some of their personal belongings before they would have to leave. While they gathered their things, the troops set fire to the guards' barracks. Then the internees marched toward Laguna de Bay."

"What about those people unable to walk?" asked Mother.

"I'm coming to that," Dad said patiently. "By this time some of the amtracs were coming into the camp." Stopping Carole's question before it was uttered, he said, "Amtracs are like large tanks, but they can go through water like ships. They loaded the sick into those machines and headed back for the lake. Those who had walked to the beach were loaded into amtracs at the water's edge."

"It must have taken hours to do all that," I put in. "There were over two thousand people at Los Banos."

"They tell me it took only forty minutes, start to finish," Dad told us with awe. "They even took the time to burn the internees' barracks. They burned everything."

"You mean Auntie and Uncle Dick rode across the lake in one of those tank-boats?" asked Carole a little enviously. "That sounds like a lot of fun."

"I guess everyone there rode out in an amtrac. It was a dangerous operation. Two of the amtracs were sunk, but fortunately everyone got out alive. Now all those who were prisoners at Los Banos are safe and being housed at Muntinlupa prison. So, as far as I know, Evelyn and Porter are among the rescued."

The liberation of the last of our family was a tremendous relief. Not every family interned by the Japanese came through the experience without losing someone. Although our health was far from good, we were at least alive.

A few hundred people had already been flown to the island of Leyte, where they boarded ship for the trip home. That was considered too rugged for those in very poor health. Mother was still about three or four weeks from her delivery date, so we waited with the rest of the camp for a ship to come for us. Since Manila Bay was not yet free of mines, it might be some time before we could leave.

By the first of March the enemy was finally driven out of Manila; it had taken almost a month. While many months would pass before the last holdouts were driven from the remote jungles, it was now safe for us to leave Santo Tomas for a few hours. Thanks to a friend Dad had made, a young American captain, we were able to see the city. He invited us to ride around town with him in his jeep.

Looking like the wasted battlefield it had been, the city was hardly habitable. We rode in stunned silence. The destruction was unbelievable. People were sorting through the rubble like zombies, bravely trying to bring order out of chaos. We could easily see what an enormous task rebuilding would be.

After only a few blocks I could no longer see the ruin and devastation; my vision was blurred by tears. I turned my sight inward, where I thought I could recall any scene from the past that I wished. But those mental pictures, too, were blurred; three years of war and imprisonment had all but erased them from memory.

The jeep stopped. Jarred from my empty dream, I looked around wondering where we were. There was nothing to see here but more rubble. Then I heard Dad speak to the captain. "If I haven't made a mistake in all this chaos, this is where we used to live," he said, pointing to a huge mound of debris. "Right there is the front step!"

Dad has made a mistake, I thought. Climbing out of the jeep, I walked dazedly toward the step. "This isn't where we lived," I murmured with certainty.

"Yes, I'm afraid it is," Dad said kindly, walking up to stand beside me. "I thought if somehow our home had survived, we might . . ." His voice trailed off in dismay.

It sounded as if he might have been thinking of perhaps refusing repatriation and remaining in Manila to rebuild our lives. But how could he? Why would he want to try? I wanted to get away from this horrible, ravaged place—to go someplace where war could never reach us again.

"I'm ready to go back to the States," I told him with uncharacteristic forthrightness. My mind was made up. "There is nothing left for us here."

"I've just about come to that conclusion too," Dad said sadly. "Come on." He tenderly took my hand. "Let's go."

Mother put her arms around Carole and me as we rode back to camp. "You girls are going to love being back in Kansas City. We can visit Grandad and Grandma Haley anytime. Your dad can find a job he really likes. In many ways, it'll be an improvement over Manila. You'll see," she promised.

I can only guess what her cheeriness cost her in effort, but in truth, I think not a great deal. Mother's priorities were properly aligned; she placed more value in her loved ones than in things. The loss of all her worldly goods seemed of no consequence to her. Dad, perhaps, mourned a way of life more than the loss of home or job. He hadn't really liked his job at the insurance company, had longed instead for a job where he could work with his hands.

Acknowledging that there would be no going back to a prewar life in the Philippines was the first step toward coming to terms with the past three years. After that we all became anxious for an early sailing date. But several weeks went by and still no ship came for us. Of course the war was still in progress, so the United States government had more things to think about than bringing home a few thousand of its far-flung citizens.

After breakfast on March 27, Mother instructed Carole and me to take care of Pete for the rest of the day, or until Dad returned. It was time for the baby! With her arm hooked through Dad's for support, they walked the short distance to the army field hospital. Dad came back to the shanty at suppertime and told us to put Pete to bed at his regular time, saying if the baby came after our bedtime he would wait until morning to bring us the news.

"Daddy! Daddy!" Pete called, waking me. He was pointing out the window, where Dad was waving.

Leaning out the window, I asked, "What is it, Dad?"

"A boy," he said proudly, "born at nine thirty last night."

"How's Mother?" Carole asked, pushing hair out of her eyes. "When can we see them?"

"Your mother is very tired," Dad told us with concern. "So we'll let her rest until afternoon."

"She'll be okay, won't she?" I asked anxiously.

"Yes," he said firmly. "The doctor said she'll be fine in a week or two. But she will need our help."

That afternoon Carole and I went to see her, while Dad stayed with Pete. We were amazed to find her walking in the hall, carrying the baby. "Mother, let me carry him," I said. "You look too tired to be out of bed!"

She said she was feeling better with every passing hour. "The doctors and nurses say I must practice walking with the baby in case we have to be evacuated." She pulled the blanket back so we could see the sleeping baby. "Meet your new baby brother," she whispered. "Isn't he a handsome little fellow?"

This time I beat Carole to the punch, when I asked, "How soon can I hold him?"

"Let's go back to my room. I am kind of tired," she admitted. "Then you girls can hold him all you like."

"Have you named him yet?" Carole asked.

"Dad and I have just about decided on Thomas Freeman," Mother told us. "What do you two girls think of that?"

"That's a good name," I said. "We can call him Tommy."

"You didn't name him after this prison camp, did you?" asked Carole doubtfully.

"No," laughed Mother. "We just like the name Thomas. And Freeman is your grandad Haley's first name, as you know."

Mother continued to rest and gain strength in the hospital. The doctors thought she should remain there until time for us to board ship for the States, although she did come one afternoon to help us sort things for packing. We stayed half ready for days. On April 8 we received word that we would be leaving the next day.

Early the next morning we assembled in front of the main building, where we boarded busses. The annual hot season was in full swing, so it felt good to be stirring up a breeze as we rode down to the port area. Once there, we could see the piers were so badly damaged that we wouldn't be able to board our ship from any of them. Instead, we walked down the beach into a strange boat with deep sides.

Dad was helping Mother, Carole had a tight grip on Pete's hand, and Tommy, not two weeks old, was all wrapped up in my arms.

"This is a funny kind of boat," I said to a sailor nearby. "What is it called?"

"LST," he answered. "It's a landing ship tank, ma'am." The sailor couldn't have been more than two or three years older than I. Why would he address me as ma'am? Did he think Tommy was my baby? I had to laugh to myself.

Mother was chuckling, too, as she said, "Here, Georgia. I'll take Tommy now."

Which of those big ships out in the bay would take us back to the States, I wondered as the LST headed across the bay. Bow spray stung my face, as my hair whipped wildly in the quickening breeze. Thoughts raced through my mind as the thrill of actually beginning our homeward voyage swelled my heart. What would it be like, living in the States?

It was the USS Cape Mears we pulled alongside. Because we had to climb a steep set of rope stairs to the deck, two sailors took the little ones. Once topside, we were taken to our quarters. Dad and Pete would bunk on a deck deep inside the ship. Carole and I were assigned to a deck with other female passengers. Mother and Tommy were given one of the few available cabins on the main deck.

The next day as the ship weighed anchor, I stood at the stem for a long time watching Manila recede in the distance. With an ache in my chest, I said good-bye to the only home I could remember. Then, resolutely, I turned and went forward to the bow. Up ahead, beyond Corregidor, the open sea and a new life beckoned to me.

Epilogue

"Well," I said with a sigh of relief, "that's the end of my story. The end of the Barnes saga." I had been relating my wartime experiences over a period of several weeks and was pleased to have reached the end. Bobbie had been a good listener, with an endless supply of probing questions.

"What a story!" she said in amazement. "You ought to write a book."

"The best time for that has probably passed," I told her. "I think my memory of those years is gradually fading. And besides, I'm thinking of starting college in the near future. I wouldn't have time for a writing project if I do that."

"What you've told me seems complete enough," Bobbie replied. "And I'm sure others would find it as engrossing as I have. Why, look at how widely read the story about Anne Frank has been these many years. Yours would be too."

I thought about that for a moment, beginning to catch her enthusiasm. "But, Bobbie," I said, "there are some very important differences between Anne Frank's story and mine. First of all, she kept a diary during the time she and her family were in hiding from the Nazis and the horror of the Holocaust. She related events with the accuracy of a reporter on the scene. I didn't keep a diary; my remembrance of events leading to and during imprisonment is growing dimmer with each passing year. Secondly, she wrote of her life in confinement with the insight of an innocent young girl. Any insight I might bring to my tale would be in retrospect, through the eyes of a grown woman. And thirdly, she bared her soul, not knowing that millions of people would someday read her diary. I think I'm too private a person to knowingly do that for publication."

"Yes, I understand the differences and your need for privacy, but I still think you should write a book," reiterated Bobbie.

"Thanks for the vote of confidence," I told her kindly. "I appreciate that. Maybe in a few years, when I run out of anything else worth doing, I might give it a try."

"Good! Now, with that near-promise, there's still a couple of things I'm wondering about. Feel like another question or two?" asked Bobbies hopefully.

"Sure."

"How do you think being in a concentration camp for such a long time has changed you?"

"That's a tough one. On the one hand, I don't know what kind of a person I might have been without that experience," I answered thoughtfully. "On the other hand, I probably am unaware of some of the changes I have gone through. Little things like cutting pies, cakes, or breads in pieces so small as to seem mean, saving scraps of cloth or pieces of string too small to be really useful—that sort of thing is probably a holdover from camp." Then I had to laugh. "Have you seen Dad's garage? He can't throw anything away yet."

"If that's the only effect of the war on you, I'd be very surprised," prodded Bobbie.

"To be honest, I have a thorough dislike of firearms. It made life a bit uncomfortable for me when I married into a farming family. I had to accept the fact that guns were a natural part of my husband's life. He realized after a time that I could never handle a gun myself."

After further reflection I said, "I find war movies much too upsetting to sit through, especially since they have become so real in the last few years. The violence and bloody gore are so horribly graphic that I can't subject myself to the trauma of reliving the sights, sounds, and smells of a battlefield."

To change my train of thought, I said, "Probably the most deep-seated effect of the whole experience is one I am just now beginning to recognize. I am now, and have for twenty years, been unable to live each day as it comes. Those three years in the concentration camp taught me to always look forward to the next day, the next month, the next year. When you concentrate so willfully on the future, you miss the here and now. The habit of almost ignoring the present in order to fill my thoughts with plans for the future is a habit I need to change."

Bobbie had run out of questions at last. I could see she was still mulling the whole story over, when she reminded me, "You must write this story. Don't let it be lost."

www.ingramcontent.com/pod-product-compliance
Lightning Source LLC
Chambersburg PA
CBHW051810040426
42446CB00007B/609